SUPER RED BOOK

PLYMOUT[...]

G000099256

LEGEND

▦▦▦	Motorway
▬	'A' Road
	...ad
	...r Road
	...strianised / ...icted Access
	...
	...t Up Area
– – – –	Footpath
∿	Stream
∿	River
Lock	Canal
▬■▬	Railway / Station
●	Post Office
P P+☰	Car Park / Park & Ride
C	Public Convenience
+	Place of Worship
→	One-way Street
i	Tourist Information Centre
▲8 ▲8	Adjoining Pages
▨	Area Depicting Enlarged Centre
▬	Emergency Services
▭	Industrial Buildings
▭	Leisure Buildings
▭	Education Buildings
▬	Hotels etc.
▬	Retail Buildings
▭	General Buildings
▭	Woodland
▭	Recreation Ground
▨	Cemetery

CONTENTS

Redbooks *showing the way*

...very effort has been made to verify the accuracy of information in this book but the ...ublishers cannot accept responsibility for expense or loss caused by an error or omission.

...formation that will be of assistance to the user of the maps will be welcomed.

...he representation on these maps of a road, track or path is no evidence of the existence of a ...ght of way.

...treet plans prepared and published by ESTATE PUBLICATIONS, Bridewell House, ...ENTERDEN, KENT. The Publishers acknowledge the co-operation of the local authorities of ...wns represented in this atlas.

Ordnance Survey This product includes mapping data licensed from Ordnance Survey® with the permission of the Controller of Her Majesty's Stationery Office.

...Crown Copyright All rights reserved
...Estate Publications 125-14 ISBN 1 84192 294 3 Licence number 100019031

www.ESTATE-PUBLICATIONS.co.uk

Printed by Ajanta Offset, New Delhi, India.

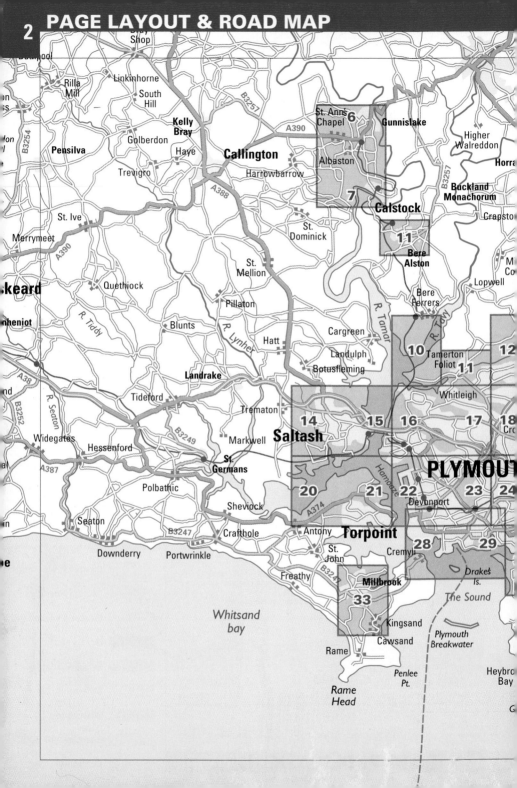

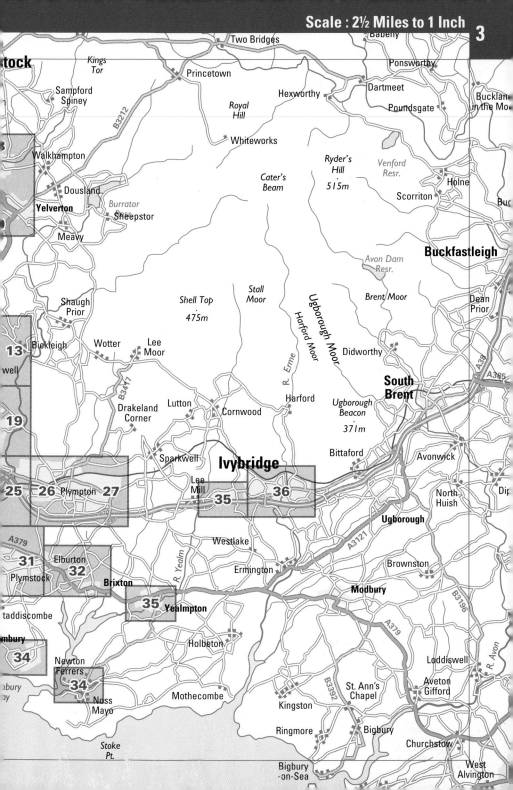

tock

Kings Tor

Two Bridges

Babeny

Ponsworthy

Princetown

Sampford Spiney

Hexworthy

Dartmeet

Poundsgate

Bucklan in the Mo

Royal Hill

Whiteworks

Walkhampton

Ryder's Hill
515m

Venford Resr.

Holne

Dousland

Burrator

Cater's Beam

Scorriton

Buc

Yelverton

Sheepstor

Avon Dam Resr.

Buckfastleigh

Meavy

Shell Top
475m

Stall Moor

Brent Moor

Dean Prior

Shaugh Prior

Bickleigh

Wotter

Lee Moor

Ugborough Moor

Harford Moor

Didworthy

13

well

R. Erme

South Brent

A385

19

Drakeland Corner

Lutton

Cornwood

Harford

Ugborough Beacon
371m

Bittaford

Avonwick

Sparkwell

Ivybridge

25

26

Plympton

27

Lee Mill

35

36

North Huish

Dip

A379

31

Elburton

32

Westlake

R. Yealm

A3121

Ugborough

Brownston

B3196

Plymstock

Brixton

35

Yealmpton

Ermington

Modbury

taddiscombe

Holbeton

Loddiswell

R. Avon

mbury

34

Newton Ferrers

34

Mothecombe

St. Ann's Chapel

B3392

Aveton Gifford

bury
ay

Noss Mayo

Kingston

A379

Stoke Pt.

Ringmore

Bigbury

Churchstow

Bigbury -on-Sea

West Alvington

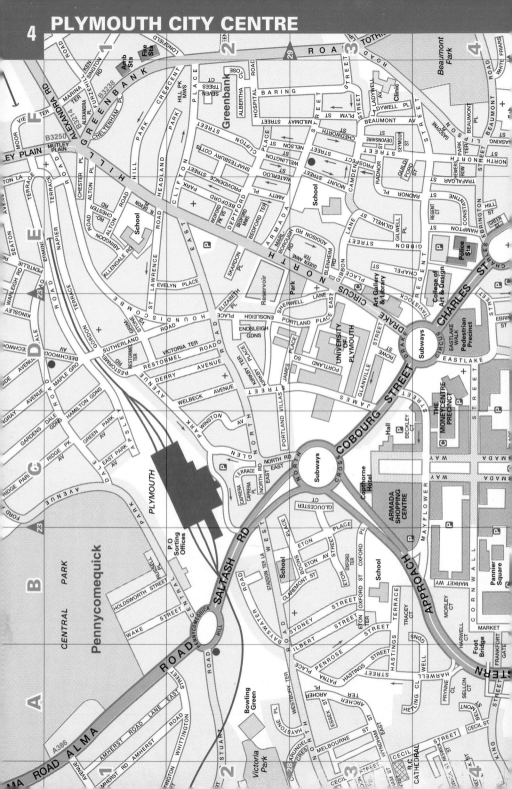

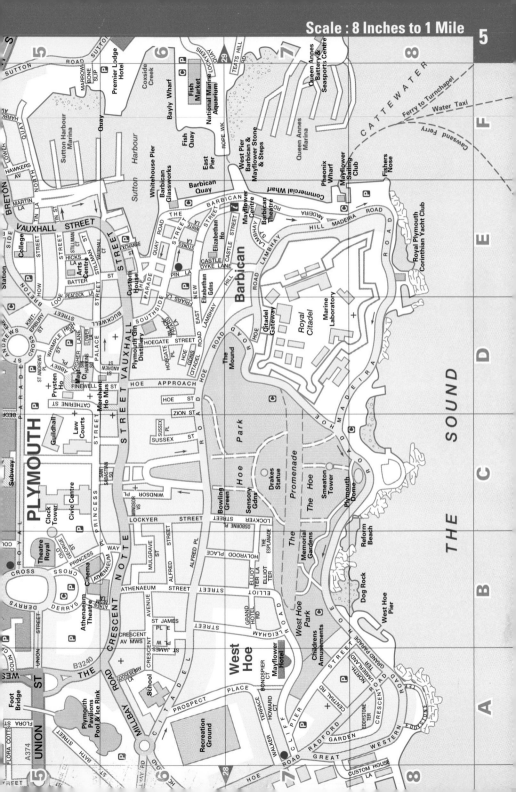

Map index labels (grid references and place names):

1 — South Bedford Mine (disused), Chimney, Shaft (dis), Hatch Wood, A390, River Tamar, New Bridge, Tip (dis)

2 — Chimney Rock, TAMAR, Weir, Tamar Canal (disused), Recreation Ground, CROCKERS ROW, KINGSWOOD RD, GAS HO LA, CLIFF VW, BEALSWOOD CL, BEALSWOOD RD, Hotel, UNDER, Hall, CALSTOCK RD, THE SQUARE, THE ORCHARD, STREET, THE CREST, FORE ST, NEWBRIDGE HILL, TAMAR TER, RUSSELL TER, COMMERCIAL RD, LISCOMBE CL, RODDA CL, RUSH PARK TER, KING, WOODLAND TER, WOODLAND WAY, BEDFORD CL, HOOPERS LANE, CHAPEL LANE, Sch, Pearsons Quarry (disused), QUARRY LANE

3 — Shaft, TAMAR, ROAD, Hatches Green, Hatches Farm, Sewage Works, Colley Cliff, CALSTOCK ROAD, LANE, Shaft (dis), GUNNISLAKE, Murifield Farm, Tamar Mills, THE PADDOCKS, ALBERT TER, Pitt Farm, Cross, WELL PARK RD, STONY, SAND HILL, Sandhill House, Higher Dimson, Lower Dimson, Shaft (dis), PARKERS GRN, Middle Dimson Farm, Sandock Nurseries, St Josephs R.C. School, Gunnislake Rural Workshops, CHAWLEIGH CT, STATION ROAD, P, Drakeswalls, DRAKEWALLS GDNS, DELAWARE CT, Delaware School, Mine (dis), Cemy, SKINNARD LANE, ROAD, MOORLAND WY, BRENTON TER, Brenton Farm, Albaston, FORE LANE, CEMETERY, WELL PARK RD

4 — Whimple Wood, Whimple, Shaft, Colley Cliff, ROAD, EDGCOMBE WY, Holiday Village

A/B/C/D/E/F (left margin):
- Tip (dis), A390, Shaft (dis)
- Shafts (dis), Quarries (dis), Wood, Clitters, Gunnislake Clitters Mine (disused), Pond
- Chimneys, Chimney (dis), Shaft (dis), Tip (dis)
- Lower Dimson, Middle Dimson, North Dimson, Gunnislake, DELAWARE ROAD, Chimney, Works, Chimney, Grays Plantation
- Chilsworthy, Hingston Down Quarries, Chimney, Roundabarrow Farm, Tumulus, Quarry (dis), Tip (dis), Shaft (dis)
- St Ann's Chapel, OLD MINE, Prospect Farm, GENNIS LANE, ALL SAINTS, S M MINE, WHITE ROCKS, PK, CL, MAWES CT, A390, Higher Brooklands, CHAPEL CL, Higher Todsworthy Farm, Todsworthy, Donkey Park, Mine (dis), Shaft (dis), Tip (dis)

Bottom row labels: **1**, **2**, **3**, **4**

Calstock
CALSTOCK
Hare Wood
Shaft (dis)
Slimeford Farm
Ravenscourt
Cemetery
CHURCH
Nurseries
Junior School
BACK RD
HAREWOOD RD
LANE
CHURCH
THE
ADIT
MARSH
Rec Grnd
Mus
Hall
FORE ST
TAMAR PL
PROVIDENCE PL
BAPTIST ST
COMMERCIAL RD
Slipway
Quay
ROWSE GDNS
STATION
ST ANDREWS CL
LANE
HILL
CHURCH
JOHNSON PK
LANE
LANG GDNS
KELLY
Buttspill
Buttspill Wood
Ferry Farm
Nurseries
Rock Park Villas
Northpark Farm
Chimney
Northpark House
Wheal Edward (dis)
SAND
PARK HILL TER
HIGHER
COTEHELE VW
TAMAR TER
TAMAR
RIVER
Glenver House
North Ward Farm
Sch
Shaft (dis)
Mine (dis)
Chimney
Tip (dis)
Hotel
LOWER
Chapel
Cotehele Wood
Mus
Tower
Reservoir
Dovecote (Remains of)
NATIONAL TRUST
Cotehele House
Cotehele Quay
Mine (dis)
Chimney
Danescoombe
Quarries (dis)
Norris Green
Newton
Newton Farm
Cotehele Mill
Comfort Wood
NICHOLAS MDW
Metherell
Sewage Works
Park View
OAKEY
ORCHARD
Clampits
Newhouses
Boars Bridge
Morden Farm
5
6
7
8
A
B
C
D
E
F

Horrabridge

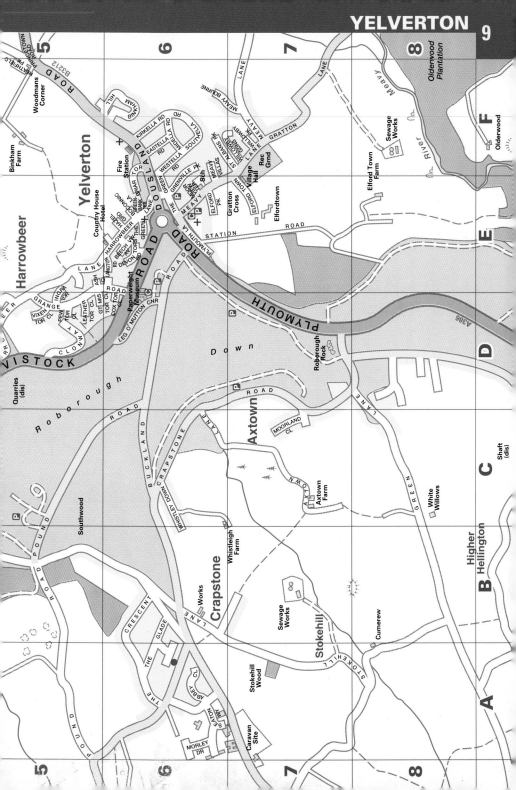

A
B
C
D

BERE FERRERS

STATION ROAD

SILVER ST

HENSBURY LA

Bere
Barton

Bere Ferrers

1

New Barn
Farm

2

T
A
V
Y

Pennards
Point

R
I
V
E
R

Warren
Plantations

3

R
I
V
E
R

Warren

Warleigh
Barton

4

Warleigh
Quay

Warleigh
House

Tavy Bridge

T
A
M
A
R

Park
Plantations

Reedwell
Plantation

5

Warleigh Point
(Nature Reserve)

Pennylake
Pond

Warleigh   Wood

Tor
Plantatio

Tor Rock

6

STATION

Badgers Park
Wood

Warren
Point

Works

Tamerton
Bridge

Woodlands
Farm

Woodlands
House

ROAD   STATION   ROAD   STATION

A
B
C
D

16

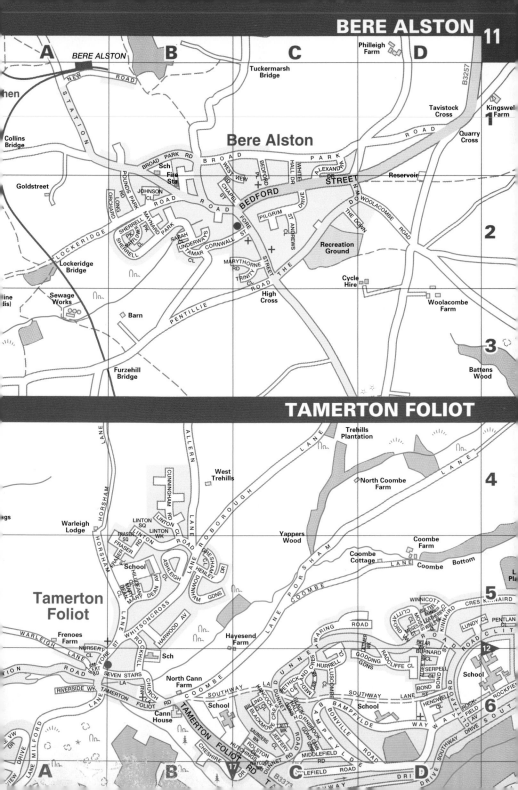

A
BERE ALSTON
B
C
Philleigh Farm
D

hen
NEW ROAD
STATION ROAD
Tuckermarsh Bridge
Tavistock Cross
Kingswell Farm
1
Collins Bridge
Bere Alston
ROAD
Quarry Cross
B3257

Goldstreet
POUNDS PARK RD
LONG ORCHARD
BROAD PARK RD
Sch
Fire Sta
JOHNSON CL
ROAD
WEST VIEW
BROAD ROAD
CHAPEL ST
BEDFORD PL
BEDFORD RD
HALL DR
WHITE
PARK
LEXANDR RD
STREET
Reservoir
WOOLACOMBE ROAD

SHERRELL RD
PK
MAYNARD PARK
SHERRELL
UNDERWAYS
SARAH CL
TAMAR
CORNWALL CL
FORE ST
PILGRIM
ST ANDREWS CL
THE DOWN
Recreation Ground
2

LOCKERIDGE
Lockeridge Bridge
MARYTHORNE RD
TRINITY CL
CORNWALL STREET
High Cross
THE
Cycle Hire
Woolacombe Farm

(line dis)
Sewage Works
Barn
PENTILLIE
Battens Wood
3

Furzehill Bridge

LANE
ALLERN LANE
LANE
Trehills Plantation
LANE
4

West Trehills
North Coombe Farm

ags
HORSHAM
Warleigh Lodge
CUNNINGHAM RD
LINTON SQ
LINTON WK
LINTON CL
FRASER SQ
FRASER
ROAD
ASHLEIGH
LANE ROBOROUGH
GRESHAM DR
HENLEY
DOWNHAM
Yappers Wood
Coombe Cottage
LANE
PORSHAM
Coombe Farm
Coombe Bottom
L Pla

Tamerton Foliot
School
HILLSIDE
MARY DEAN AV
MARY DEAN
WHITSONCROSS
HARWOOD AV
COOMBE
WINNICOTT
CLIFFORD
KINNAIRD
CRES KINNAIRD
LUNDY CL
PENTLAND CL
CLIT
12
5

WARLEIGH LANE
Frenoes Farm
NURSERY CL
ALBERT RD
FORE ST
SEVEN STARS LA
ROCKHILL
Sch
Hayesend Farm
WARING
ROAD
PILLAR
BURNARD
GODDING GDNS
RADCLIFFE CL
SERPELL
BOND ST
School
6

RIVERSIDE WK
TAMERTON FOLIOT
CHURCH RD
North Cann Farm
School
DUNNET
HURRELL
LUSCOMBE
BETHICK
SOUTHWAY LANE
BONVILLE
HENDWELFORD CL
ROCKFIELD
Cann House
SOUTHWAY
BILLING CRES
BLACKTHORN
SAUNDERS WK
ROLSTON
MIDDLEFIELD RD
BAMPFYLDE
WAY WAYFORD
SOUTHWAY DRIVE

VIEW VW
DRIVE
LANE MILFORD
TAMERTON FOLIOT RD
CHESHIRE
17
B3373
LEFIELD ROAD
DRI
DRIVE
SOUT

A
B
C
D

ROBOROUGH

A · B · C · D

1

Bame Wood

North Broadley
Coppers

BACK LANE

Broadley

Haxter Lodge

Roborough Plantations

Roborough Reservoir

NATION TRUS

A386

2

sburgh Wood

Dunsburgh Farm

PARKWOOD CL

PARK

TAMERTON ROAD

Roborough Farm

INDUSTRIAL PARK

Roborough House

LEIGH

11

BROADLEY

Haxter Wood

NEW RO

Hall

3

Porsham Plantation

Ten Acre Brake

Porsham

HAXTER CL

PORSHAM CL

BELLIVER INDUSTRIAL ESTATE

BELLIVER

WAY ROAD

Reservoir (covered)

Belliver

TAVISTOCK

LOPES RD

TYNE GORE

LEAT WK

AGE CR

CARRON WALK

WALK

CARRON RD

4

Porsham

LANE

Porsham Coppice

Arnold's Hill Coppice

Belliver Coppice

Widewell Wood

BELLIVER

LEGIS WK

INGRA WK

HESSARY

STAPLE CL

LEGIS AV

BOULTER CL

DRIVE

CRAMBER CL

Roborough

BOLTER DRIVE

TAVISTOCK CR

LUMP

YOKENEY

BICKLEIGH DOWN

Foot Bridge

DRIVE

BUSIN PAR

Off

11

Porsham Wood

The Brake

BEVERSTON WAY

BEVERSTON

BARBURY CRES

TREAGO GDNS

CALDICOT GDNS

TIVERTON CL

WIDEWELL LA

CHEDSTON WAY

ROAD

WOOLWELL CRES

TORFIELD DRIVE

WOOLWELL

Superstore

WOOLWELL

COPPICE

BEECH CL

HAWTHORN

FORRESTERS DR

SILVER

RIVER FORD DR

OAKLANDS DR

SYCAMORE DR

WARRE

5

Bottom

Langley Plantation

KINNAIRD

CRES

LUNDY CL

PENTLAND CL

STROMA CL

SKERRIES

CLITTAFORD

LANGLEY CRES

LIZARD CL

LIZARD WK

CROMER WK

CRESCENT

BARHILL

BARHILL RD

Warehouses

Factory

Works

HIGHCLERE GDNS

HOLNE CHASE

PRESTON

BURY CL

DRIVE

TIVERTON CL

WAR

DOUR CL

HEDINGHAM GDNS

WIDEWELL LA

Sch

Widewell

WIDEWELL RD

WIDEWELL RD

ROAD

FRENSHAM AV

FRENSHAM

AVENUE

THE COURT

THE FANCY

BUENA

CROMWELL GATE

VISTA CL

VISTA GDNS

BUENA VISTA DRIVE

BUENA VISTA CL

BUENA VISTA WY

HOLTWOOD

6

School

CRES

INCHKEITH

ROAD

CLITTAFORD RD

ALDERNEY RD

SKERRIES RD

Library

BOROUGH ROAD

FLAM

LONGSTONE AVENUE

PENDEEN

GOODWIN

PENDEEN

AVENUE

CRESCENT

BRAMBLE WK

FREWIN

School

Factory

LULWORTH

LAUNCESTON

SOUTHWAY

SOUTHWAY DRIVE

BARNINGHAM

BARNDALE

BARNDALE AV

HAZEL CL

FARNLEY

FARNLEY

OLDLANDS

DAVE

NHAM

CRES

TYNE

CORSHAM

GDNS

CL

WORLEY

BURTON

BROCKTON

EAST COTE

ABBEY

COLSTON CL

Ridin School

VISTA

VISTA CL

ST ANNES CL

WESTWOOD

GLENFIELD

School

ROCKFIELD AVENUE

SOUTHWAY DRIVE

Southway

PLYMBRIDGE ROAD

TAVISTOCK

ROAD PA

18

A · B · C · D

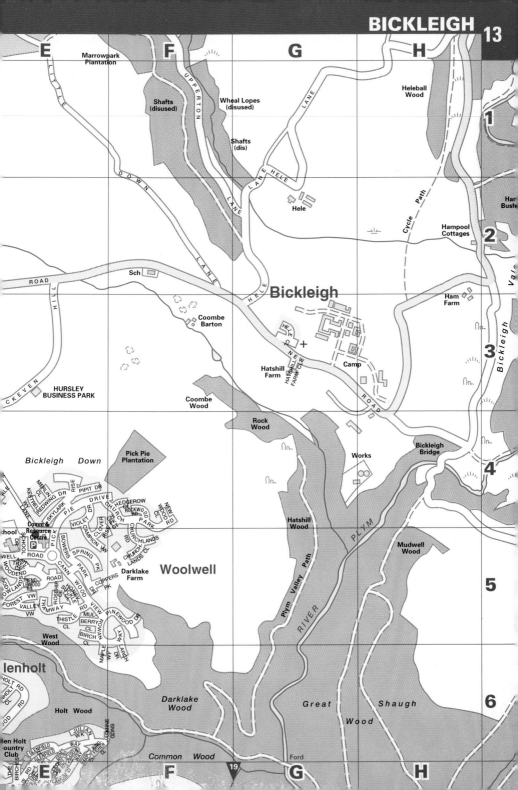

E **F** **G** **H**

Marrowpark Plantation

LITTLE DOWN HILL

UPPERTON LANE

Shafts (disused)

Wheal Lopes (disused)

Shafts (dis)

LANE

HELE LANE

Heleball Wood

1

Hele

Cycle Path

Har Bush

ROAD

LANE

Sch

Coombe Barton

HELE

Hampool Cottages

2

Bickleigh

Ham Farm

CKEVEN HILL

HURSLEY BUSINESS PARK

Hatshill Farm

HATSHILL FARM CL

NEW

+

Camp

3

Coombe Wood

Rock Wood

NEW ROAD

Bickleigh Bridge

4

Bickleigh   Down

Pick Pie Plantation

Works

Bickleigh Vale

Pearl School

Comm & Resource Centre

MERLIN CL

KESTREL WYNNE

REDWING DR

SKYLARK

PIPIT DR

RISE

PIE DRIVE

CHURCH RD

ROCKWOOD RD

NEW WOOD RD

PARK

HEDGEROW

VIOLET CL

CLOVER

CAMPION VW

CHURCHLANDS RD

Hatshill Wood

Mudwell Wood

WELL DR

WOODEND

FOREST VW

DOWLAND

STRENO LEWOOD RD

BOWERS CL

CANN WOOD

SPRING PK

TREE CL

PARK ROAD

CHURCH LANDS CL

Darklake Farm

Woolwell

PLYM VALLEY PATH

RIVER   PLYM

5

THE BIRCHES

VALLEY VW

TRAMWAY

SCHOOL DR

THISTLE CL

MUL CL

BERRY CL

BIRCH CL

POMROY AVE

PINEWOOD RD

MAPLE RD

LARCH DR

COPPERS PK

West Wood

lenholt

HOLT RD

Holt Wood

Darklake Wood

Great   Shaugh

Wood

6

en Holt ountry Club

GLENFIELD

JULIAN WK

JASMINE GDNS

WAY

Common   Wood

Ford

▼ **19**

E **F** **G** **H**

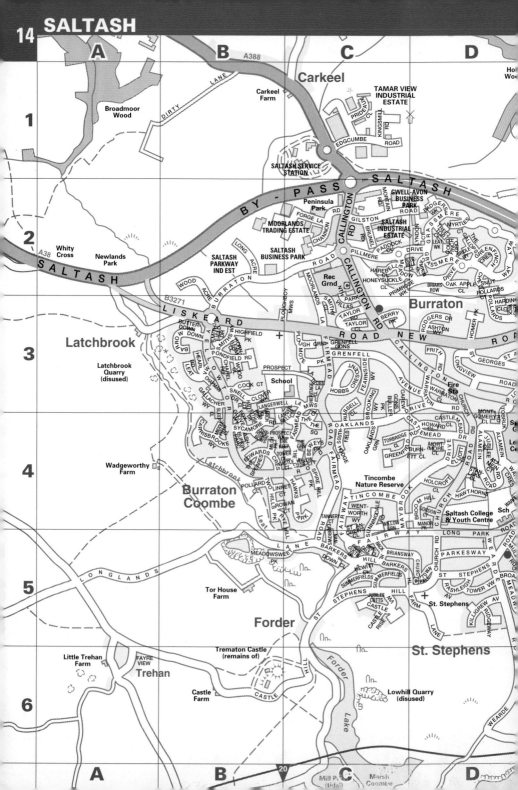

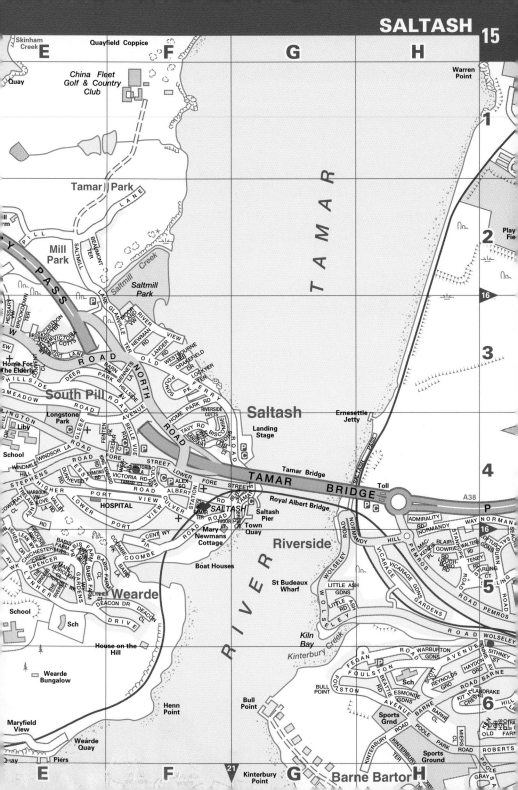

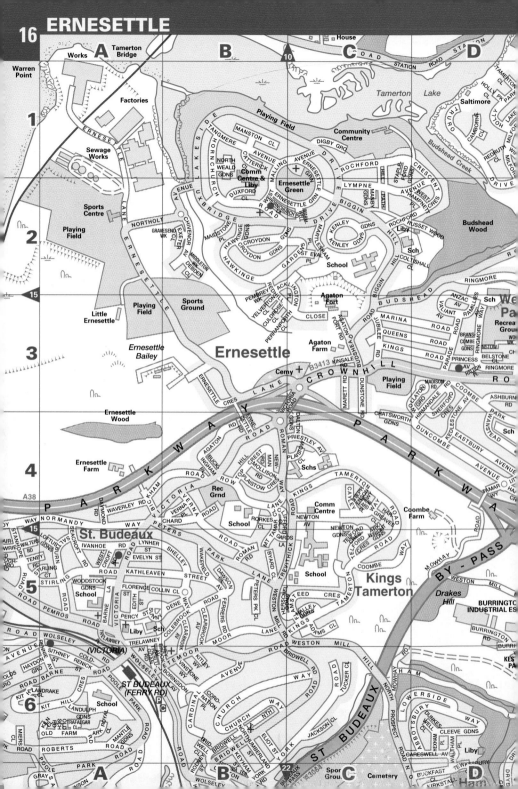

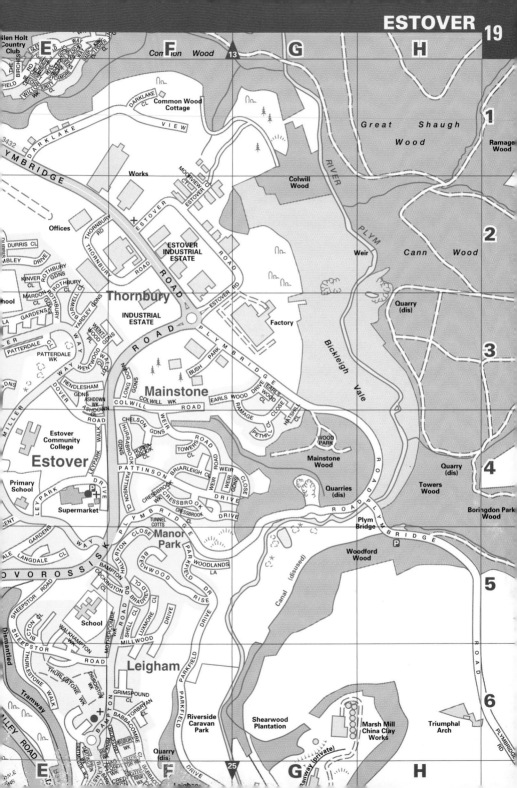

E F G H

Glen Holt Country Club

Com on Wood 13

Great Shaugh Wood

Ramage Wood

1

DARKLAKE CL

Common Wood Cottage

VIEW

3432

RYMBRIDGE

DARKLAKE

Works

MOORVIEW CL

ESTOVER CL

Colwill Wood

RIVER

PLYM

Cann Wood

2

Offices

THORNBURY RD

THORNBURY

ROAD

ESTOVER ROAD

ESTOVER INDUSTRIAL ESTATE

Weir

Quarry (dis)

DURRIS CL

MBLEY DRIVE

KINVER CL

ROTHBURY GDNS

ROTHBURY CL

MARDON CL

YURWELL

YARDLEY GDNS

WENTWOOD PL

WENTWOOD CL

ROAD

ROAD

Factory

ESTOVER RD

Thornbury

INDUSTRIAL ESTATE

PLYMBRIDGE

Bickleigh Vale

3

school

GARDENS

PATTERDALE

PATTERDALE WK

WAY

HENDLESHAM GDNS

ASHDOWN WK

ASHDOWN CL

ROAD

NROD

SNGD

COLWILL WK

Mainstone

COLWILL ROAD

BUSH PARK

EARLS WOOD DRIVE

EARLS WOOD CL

RAMAGE

HATSHILL

PETHILL

WOOD PARK

Quarry (dis)

4

DNS

MILLER

DOVER

WAY

CHELSON GDNS

HURRABROOK GDNS

HURRABROOK

TOWER CL

ROAD

WEIR

BRIARLEIGH CL

WEIR ROAD

WEIR CLOSE

WOOD CLOSE

DRIVE

Mainstone Wood

Towers Wood

Quarry (dis)

Estover Community College

Estover

PATTINSON DRIVE

PATTINSON CL

CRESSBROOK WK

CRESSBROOK

CRESSBROOK DRIVE

ROAD PLYM

Quarries (dis)

Boringdon Park Wood

Primary School

LEYPARK WALK

LEYPARK DRIVE

P

Supermarket

TUNNEL COTTS

PLYMBRIDGE

Plym Bridge

P

Woodford Wood

BRIDGE

ROAD

5

NOVOROSSISK

GARDENS

LANGDALE CL

WAY

Manor Park

ELBURTON CLOSE

BAMPTON

BEECHWOOD

COCKINGTON CL

BRADLEY ROAD

SHELL CL

WOODLANDS LA

PARKFIELD DR RISE

LUXMORE DRIVE

Canal (disused)

LE

ALE

DISMANTLED

SHEEPSTOR CL

BICTON CL

WALKHAMPTON

MOTHERCOMBE WK

MILLWOOD

School

ROAD

6

Tramway

THURLESTONE WK

THURLESTONE WALK

Leigham

PHURSTON WK

BAMPTON

GRIMSPOUND CL

BABBACOMBE WK

TORBRYAN CL

PARKFIELD DRIVE

PARKFIELD

Riverside Caravan Park

Shearwood Plantation

Railway (private)

Marsh Mill China Clay Works

Triumphal Arch

PLYMBRIDGE RD

ROAD

VALLEY ROAD

Dismantled

Quarry (dis)

Leigham

25

E F G H

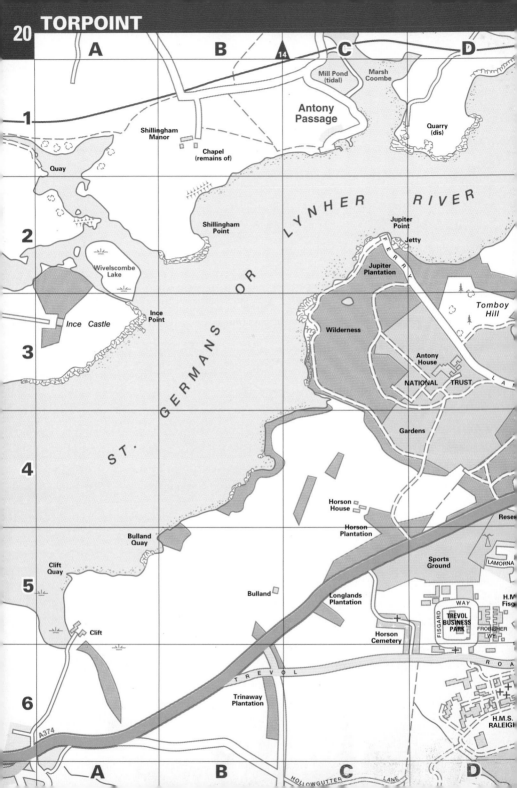

A **B** 14 **C** **D**

Mill Pond (tidal)

Marsh Coombe

Antony Passage

Quarry (dis)

Shillingham Manor

Chapel (remains of)

1

Quay

L Y N H E R   R I V E R

Shillingham Point

Jupiter Point

Jetty

2

Wivelscombe Lake

Jupiter Plantation

Tomboy Hill

Ince Point

Wilderness

Ince Castle

3

Antony House

NATIONAL   TRUST

S T .   G E R M A N S   O R

Gardens

4

Horson House

Reser

Horson Plantation

Bulland Quay

LAMORNA

Clift Quay

Sports Ground

H.M Fisg

5

Bulland

Longlands Plantation

TREVOL BUSINESS PARK

FROBISHER WY.

Clift

Horson Cemetery

FISGARD WAY

R O A

Trinaway Plantation

T R E V O L

H.M.S. RALEIGH

6

A374

HOLLOWGUTTER LANE

A **B** **C** **D**

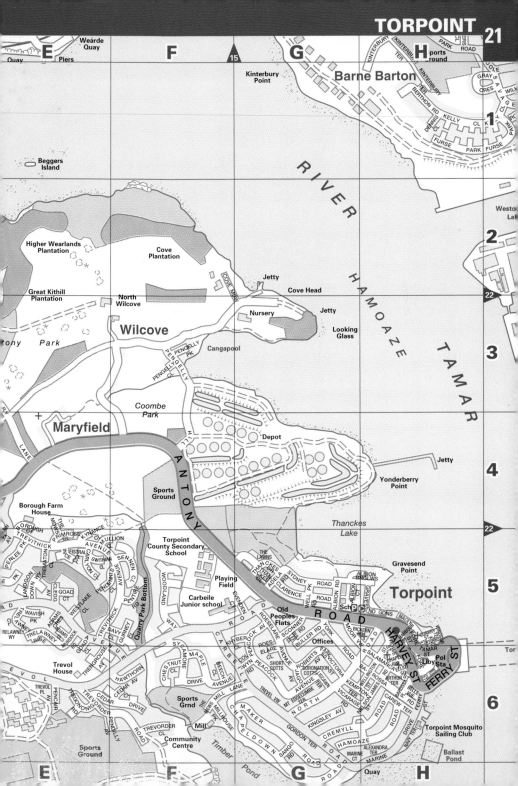

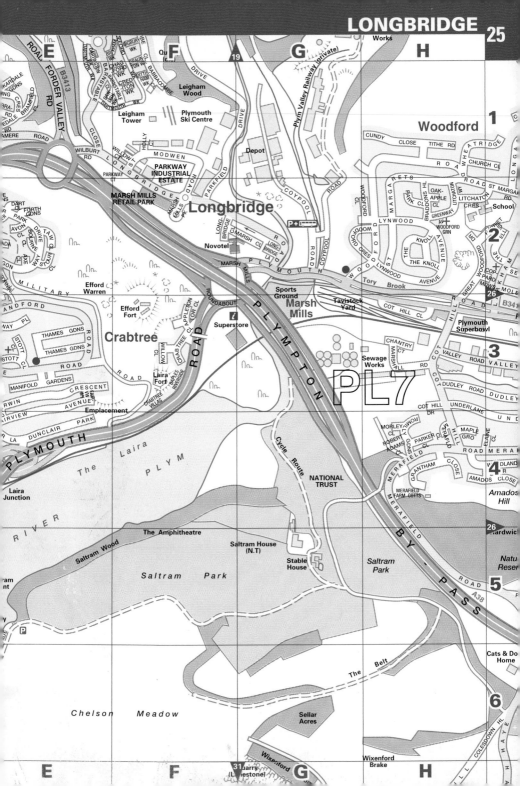

Works

E · F · G · H

Woodford

Leigham
Wood

Plym Valley Railway (private)

Leigham
Tower

Plymouth
Ski Centre

Depot

CUNDY
CLOSE

TITHE RD

WHEATRIDGE

ROAD

CHURCH CL

ST MARGA

PARKWAY
INDUSTRIAL
ESTATE

MODWEN

COYPOOL

ROAD

School

MARGARETS

OAK-
APPLE
CL

LITCHATON
CRES

**MARSH MILLS
RETAIL PARK**

Longbridge

WOODFORD

BRADONS HL

PARK

GREENWAY

AV

WOODFORD
GRN

LYNWOOD

ST

THE
KNOLL

WOODFORD AVENUE

Novotel

LONGBRIDGE

MARSH CL

LONGBRIDGE

P+

ROAD

MARSH MILLS

PLYMOUTH

WOODFORD CRES

LYNWOOD

THE KNOLL

AVENUE

ROAD

26

B341

Efford
Warren

Efford
Fort

APPLETON

ROUNDABOUT

Sports
Ground

**Marsh
Mills**

Tory Brook

Tavistock
Yard

COT HILL CL

Plymouth
Superbowl

Crabtree

THAMES GDNS

THAMES GDNS

MOTTIM

CRAB TREE

CL

PLYMPTON

ROAD

i

Superstore

CHANTRY
CT

Sewage
Works

MARSH

COT HILL

PL7

VALLEY

ROAD

VALLEY

DUDLEY

3

MANIFOLD
GARDENS

CRESCENT

AVENUE

Laira
Fort

CRABTREE
VILLAS

MARSH

RIVERSIDE

DUDLEY ROAD

COT HILL
DR

UNDERLANE

UN

Emplacement

DUNCLAIR PARK

FIRVIEW

PLYMOUTH

The Laira

PLYM

Cycle Route

MORLEY
CL

ROBERT

ADAMS

GDNS

PARKER

HERALD

MAPLE
GRO

ELAINE

ROAD

MERA

Laira
Junction

**NATIONAL
TRUST**

GRANTHAM

MERAFIELD

CLOSE

AMADOS

DLAND

CLOSE

4

MERAFIELD
FARM COTTS

Amados
Hill

RIVER

26

Hardwick

The Amphitheatre

Saltram House
(N.T)

Saltram
Park

Natu
Reser

Saltram Wood

Stable
House

Saltram Park

BY-PASS

ROAD

A38

5

Cats & Do
Home

The Belt

Chelson Meadow

Sellar
Acres

6

31 Quarry
(Limestone)

Wixenford

Wixenford
Brake

COLESDOWN HL

HAYE

E · F · G · H

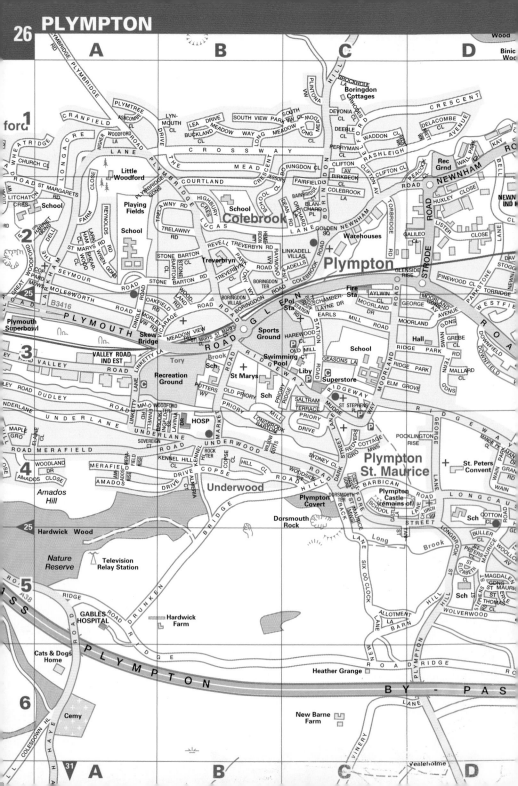

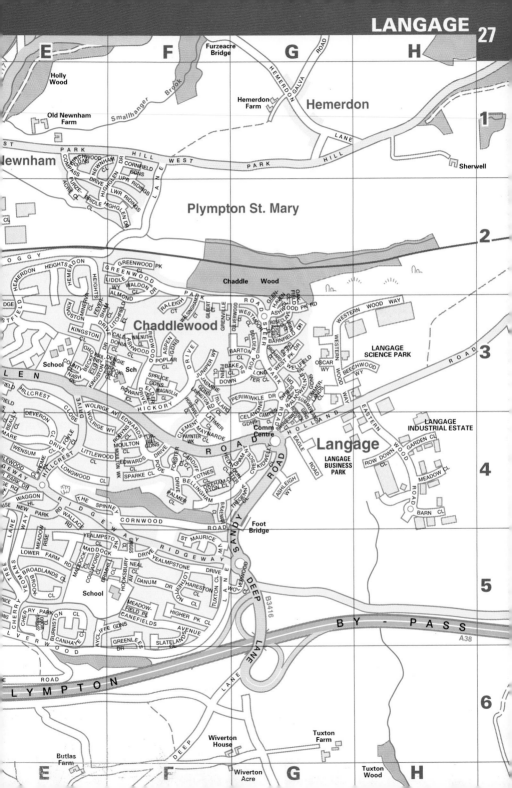

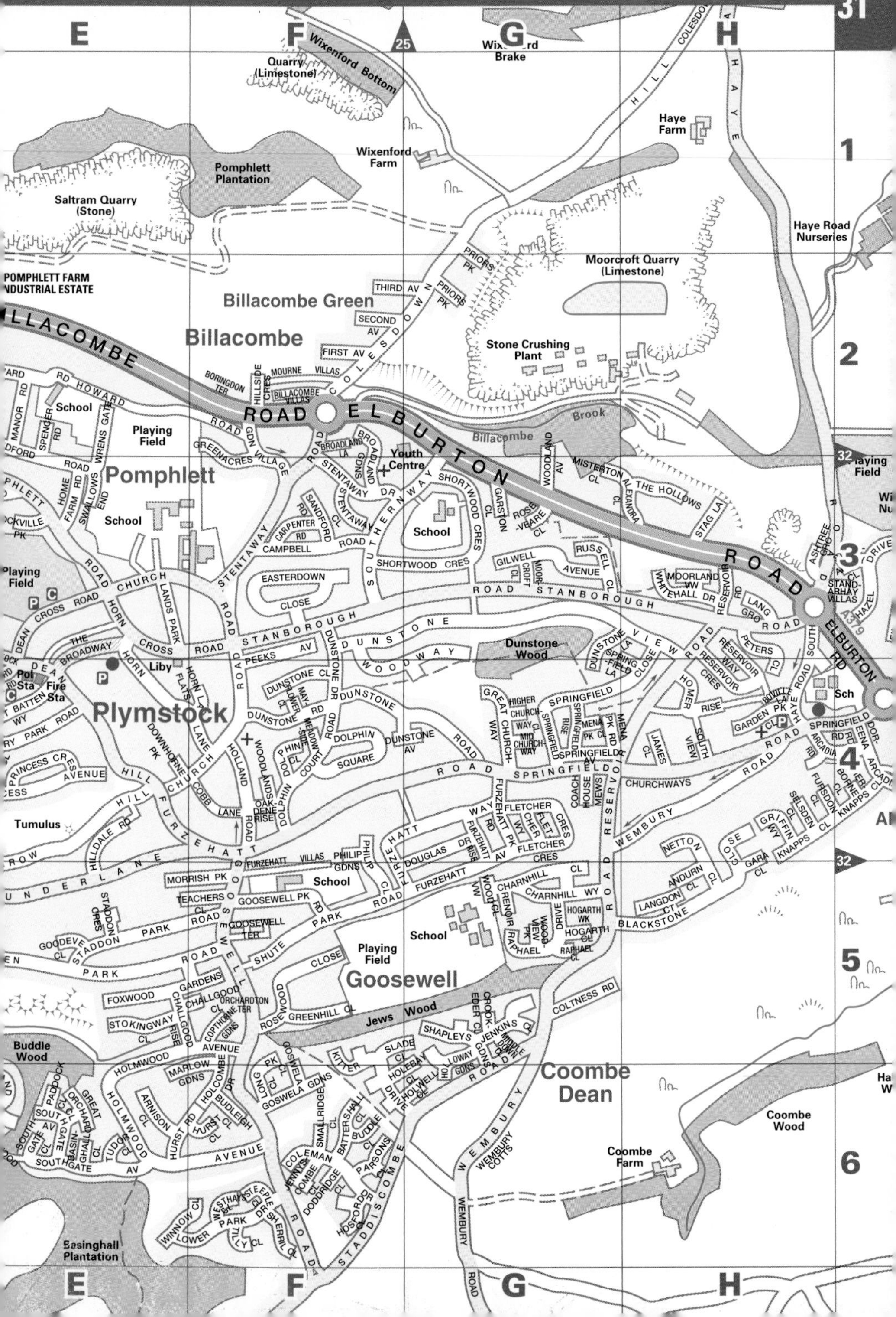
E
F
G
H
1
2
3
4
5
6
25
32
32
Wixenford Bottom
Quarry (Limestone)
Wixenford Brake
Haye Farm
Wixenford Farm
Pomphlett Plantation
Saltram Quarry (Stone)
Haye Road Nurseries
Moorcroft Quarry (Limestone)
POMPHLETT FARM INDUSTRIAL ESTATE
Billacombe Green
Billacombe
Stone Crushing Plant
BILLACOMBE ROAD
ELBURTON ROAD
Billacombe Brook
School
Playing Field
Pomphlett
Youth Centre
School
School
Playing Field
Dunstone Wood
Liby
Pol Sta
Fire Sta
Plymstock
Sch
Tumulus
School
School
Playing Field
Goosewell
Jews Wood
Buddle Wood
Coombe Dean
Coombe Wood
Coombe Farm
Easinghall Plantation
CHURCH ROAD
STANBOROUGH ROAD
DUNSTONE ROAD
SPRINGFIELD ROAD
FURZEHATT ROAD
UNDERLANE
STADDON PARK ROAD
GOOSEWELL ROAD
HOLMWOOD AVENUE
SOUTHGATE AV
STADDISCOMBE ROAD
WEMBURY ROAD
RESERVOIR ROAD
HAYE ROAD
COLESDOWN HILL
SOUTHERNWAY
STENTAWAY
HORN CROSS ROAD
THE BROADWAY
DEAN CROSS ROAD
FURZEHATT HILL
COLTNESS RD
BLACKSTONE
CHURCHWAYS
A379

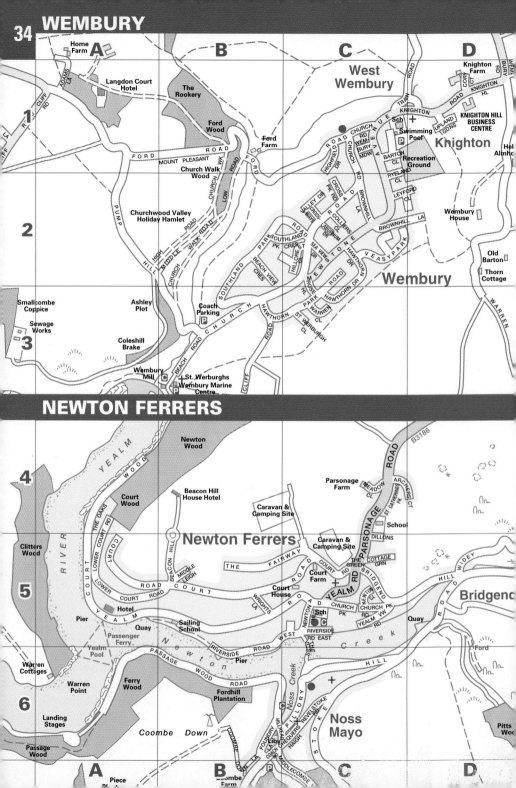

WEMBURY

A Home Farm
B
C West Wembury
D Knighton Farm

CLIFF RD
ADAMS LA
Langdon Court Hotel
The Rookery
Ford Wood
1
FORD ROAD
Ford Farm
MOUNT PLEASANT
Church Walk Wood
CHURCH WK
LOW RD
FORD RD
HIGHFIELD DR
CHURCH RD
WEM RD
CHURCH RD
WEMBURY AVENUE
TRAIN RD
KNIGHTON ROAD
Sch
CORY CT
KNIGHTON HL
WEMBURY RD
UPLAND GDNS
KNIGHTON HILL BUSINESS CENTRE
Knighton
Swimming Pool
P
BARTON CL
WEM MDW
Recreation Ground
Hel Almho

HIGH HILL
MIDDLE
CHURCH WALK ROAD
PUMP
Churchwood Valley Holiday Hamlet
SOUTHLAND ROAD
SOUTHLAND PK
HILLCRE ST
VALLEY DR
PK RD
CROSS RD
G COLLIERS
ARDUNUM DR
BROWNHILL LA
RYELAND CL
LEYFORD CL
Wembury House
BROWNHILL LA
Old Barton
Thorn Cottage
2

Smallcombe Coppice
Sewage Works
3
Ashley Plot
Coleshill Brake
Coach Parking
P
BEACH VIEW CRES
SEA VIEWS DR
W ST
VEASY PARK
HAWTHORN DR
FROST ST
ST WERBURGH CL
WARREN CL
PARK RD
HAWTHORN DR
Wembury
WARREN
CHURCH ROAD
HAWTHORN ROAD
CLIFF RD
BEACH RD
Wembury Mill
C
St. Werburghs
Wembury Marine Centre

NEWTON FERRERS

A
B Newton Wood
C Parsonage Farm
D

YEALM WOOD
RIVER YEALM
Court Wood
Beacon Hill House Hotel
Caravan & Camping Site
MEADOW CL
PARSONAGE ROAD
B3186
ST CATHERINES CT
ARCHERS CT
4

Clitters Wood
5
THE OAKS
LOWER COURT RD
COURT RD
BEACON HILL
MIDDLE LEIGH
LOWER COURT ROAD
COURT
Newton Ferrers
THE FAIRWAY
Caravan & Camping Site
School
DILLONS
THE GREEN
COTTAGE GRN
YEALM RD
Court Farm
BRIDGEND RD
NEWTON RD
HILL
WIDEY
Bridgend

Pier
Hotel
Quay
Sailing School
RIVER YEALM
Passenger Ferry
Yealm Pool
WRIGHTS LA
Court House
NEWTON RD
RD EAST
WEST
Sch
C
CHURCH PK
CHURCH RD
YEALM VW RD
Quay
ROAD HILL
Ford

Warren Cottages
Warren Point
Ferry Wood
NEWTON WOOD
PASSAGE
RIVERSIDE ROAD
Pier
RIVERSIDE RD EAST
Creek
Noss Creek
HILL
6
Landing Stages
Passage Wood
Coombe Down
COOMBE RD
Fordhill Plantation
Libr
P
FOUNDRY RD
CONSALS LA
HILLSIDE RD
CHEQUERS HILL
HAIGH
REVELSTOKE
STOKE ROAD
PILLORY HILL
Noss Mayo
Pitts Wood

A Piece
B Coombe Farm
C
D

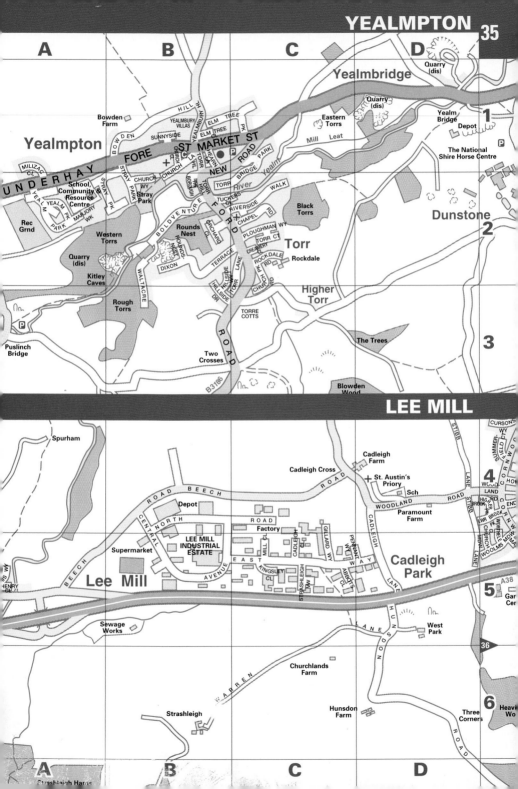

A B C D

Yealmbridge

Quarry (dis)

Bowden Farm

Yealmpton

YEALMBURY VILLAS

SUNNYSIDE

HILL

ELM TREE PK

ELM TREE

YEALMBURY HL

FORE ST ST MARKET ST

NEW ROAD

Eastern Torrs

Quarry (dis)

Yealm Bridge

Depot

The National Shire Horse Centre

1

Mill Leat

River Yealm

MILIZAC CL

UNDERHAY

YEALM PK

YEALM PK

MARJORY WK

STRAY PK

CHURCH WY

Stray Park

CHURCH

THE BOROUGH

TORR HILL

TORR

HEARN CL

BRIDGE PARK

TORR

BOLDVENTURE

FORD ROAD

WALK

Dunstone

School, Community & Resource Centre

Rec Grnd

Western Torrs

Quarry (dis)

Kitley Caves

Rounds Nest

ROUNDS NEST

DIXON

ORCHARD

RIVERSIDE

CHAPEL

PLOUGHMAN WY

CREAMERY

ROCKDALE

TORR CT

Black Torrs

Torr

Rockdale

2

WALTACRE

TERRACE

TORR LANE

HILLSIDE

TORR PK RD

CHURCH RD

Higher Torr

Rough Torrs

HILLSIDE DR

TORRE COTTS

The Trees

3

Puslinch Bridge

Two Crosses

B3186

Blowden Wood

Spurham

CURSONS

SUMMERFIELD WY

STIBB LANE

CORNWOO

Cadleigh Farm

St. Austin's Priory

Cadleigh Cross

Sch

WOOD LAND

HIGHER BROOK

PK CHURCH CL

WORTHELE MDW

WOOLMS

HO

END

4

ROAD

BEECH

ROAD

CADLEIGH ROAD

WOODLAND ROAD

Paramount Farm

Depot

NORTH ROAD

CENTRAL ROAD

Factory

LEE MILL INDUSTRIAL ESTATE

Supermarket

EAST AVENUE

MILL CL

GILARD WY

CADLEIGH

KINGSLEY CL

STRASHLEIGH VW

PENNANT WY

ABBOTS

Cadleigh Park

CADLEIGH LANE

HUNSDON LANE

A38

5

Gar Cen

36

Lee Mill

HENRY CL

S WY

BEECH

Sewage Works

West Park

WARREN

Churchlands Farm

Strashleigh

Hunsdon Farm

Three Corners

Heavi Wo

6

A B C D

Strashleigh Harris

A - Z INDEX TO STREETS
with Postcodes

The Index includes some names for which there is insufficient space on the maps. These names are indicated by an * and are followed by the nearest adjoining thoroughfare.

37

Boringdon Rd, Turnchapel PL9 30 A4
Boringdon Ter, Bodmin PL31 31 F2
Boringdon Ter, Plympton PL7 26 B2
Boringdon Ter, Turnchapel PL9 30 A4
Boringdon Villas PL7 26 B3
Borough Ct PL11 21 E4
Borough Pk PL11 21 E5
Borrowdale Cl PL6 17 G1
Boscastle Gdns PL2 17 F6
Boswell Cl PL5 17 E5
Boulden Cl PL7 27 G3
Boulter Cl PL6 12 D3
Bounds Pl PL1 29 E3
Bourne Cl PL3 25 E2
Boville La PL31 31 H4
Bowden Fm PL6 18 B5
Bowden Hill PL8 35 B1
Bowden Park Rd PL6 18 A5
Bowers Park Dr PL6 13 E5
Bowers Rd PL2 23 E3
Bowhays Walk PL6 24 C1
Boxhill Cl PL5 17 E4
Boxhill Gdns PL2 17 F6
Bracken Cl PL6 13 E4
Braddons Hill PL7 25 H2
Bradfield Cl PL6 19 F5
Bradford Cl PL6 24 B1
Bradley Rd PL4 24 A4
Braemar Cl PL7 27 F4
Brake Rd PL5 17 G4
Bramble Cl PL3 24 C2
Bramble Walk, Eggbuckland PL6 24 C1
Bramble Walk, Southway PL6 12 B6
Bramfield Pl PL6 25 E1
Bramley Rd PL3 24 D4
Brancker Rd PL2 23 F2
Brandon Rd PL3 24 D4
Brandreth Rd PL3 24 A3
Branscombe Gdns PL5 16 D3
Branson Ct PL7 27 G4
Braunton Walk PL6 25 F1
Brayford Cl PL5 17 E3
Breakwater Hill PL4 30 A2
Breakwater Ind Est PL9 30 C2
Breakwater Rd PL9 30 C2
Brean Down Cl PL3 23 H2
Brean Down Rd PL3 23 G2
Brecon Cl PL3 24 A1
Brent Knoll Rd PL3 23 G2
Brentford Av PL5 17 E1
Brenton Ter PL18 6 C4
Brentor Rd PL4 30 B1
Brest Rd PL6 18 B2
Brest Way PL6 18 B3
Breton Side PL1,4 5 E5
Brett Walk PL7 26 D1
Briansway PL12 14 C5
Briar Rd PL3 24 A2
Briar Tor PL20 9 E6
Briardale Rd PL2 22 C2
Briarleigh Cl PL6 19 F4
Briars Row PL12 14 D2
Bridge Pk PL21 36 D2
Bridge Rd PL4 30 B1
Bridgend Hill PL8 34 C5
Bridgwater Cl PL6 18 B6
Bridle Cl PL7 27 E2
Bridle Way PL12 14 D2
Bridwell Cl PL5 16 B6
Bridwell La North PL5 16 B6
Bridwell Rd PL5 16 B6
Brimhill Cl PL7 27 E5
Brismar Walk PL6 24 C1
Britannia Pl PL4 30 B1
Brixham Walk PL6 19 E6
Brixton Rd PL8 32 B3
Broad Park Rd, Plymouth PL3 23 G3
Broad Park Rd, Yelverton PL20 11 B1
Broad Pk PL9 30 C4
Broad Walk PL12 14 D5
Broadland Gdns PL31 31 F2
Broadland La PL31 31 F2
Broadlands Cl PL7 27 E5
Broadley Park Rd PL6 12 B2
Brockhole La PL7 26 C1
Brockley Rd PL3 24 C4
Brockton Gdns PL6 12 C6
Bromhead Ct PL6 18 A6
Bromley Pl PL2 22 D4
Bronte Pl PL5 17 G6
Brook Cl PL7 27 E5
Brook Rd PL21 36 D3
Brookdown Ter PL12 15 E3
Brookdown Villas PL12 15 E3
Brooke Cl PL12 15 G4
Brookfield Cl PL7 27 E3
Brooking Cl PL6 18 B6
Brooking Way PL12 14 C4
Brookingfield Cl PL7 26 B4
Brooklands PL6 17 H3
Brooks Hill PL12 15 E2
Brookwood Rd PL9 32 B2
Broom Hill PL12 14 D4
Broom Pk PL9 30 C5
Broomfield Dr PL9 30 C5
Broughton Cl PL3 23 H1
Brownhill La PL9 34 C2
Browning Rd PL2 22 D4
Brownlow St PL1 28 D3
Broxton Dr PL9 30 D2
Brunel Av PL2 22 C3
Brunel Rd PL12 14 C2
Brunel Ter PL2 22 C3
Brunel Way PL21 36 E2
Brunswick Pl PL2 22 C5
Brunswick Rd PL4 30 A1
Brynmoor Cl PL3 24 B2
Brynmoor Pk PL3 24 B2
Brynmoor Walk PL3 24 B2
Buckfast Cl, Ivybridge PL21 36 D3
Buckfast Cl, Plymouth PL2 22 D1
Buckingham Pl PL5 16 B4
Buckland Cl PL7 26 B1
Buckland Rd PL20 9 C6
Buckwell St PL1 5 D6
Buddle Cl, Bodmin PL31 31 F6
Buddle Cl, Ivybridge PL21 36 E2
Budleigh Cl PL31 31 F6
Budshead Grn PL5 17 F2
Budshead Rd PL5 16 C3
Budshead Way PL6 17 H4
Buena Vista Cl PL6 12 D6
Buena Vista Dr PL6 12 D6
Buena Vista Gdns PL6 12 D6
Buena Vista Way PL6 12 D6
Bull Point PL5 15 G6
Bulleid Cl PL2 22 C2
Buller Cl, Plymouth PL7 26 D5
Buller Cl, Torpoint PL11 21 G5
Buller Pk PL12 14 C3
Buller Rd PL11 21 G5
Bulmer Rd PL4 24 B6
Bulteel Gdns PL6 11 D5
Bunyan Cl PL5 17 F4
Burleigh La PL3 23 G2
Burleigh Manor PL3 23 G1
Burleigh Park Rd PL3 23 G2
Burnard Cl PL6 11 D6
Burnett Cl PL12 14 D4
Burnett Rd PL6 17 H6
Burnham Park Rd PL3 23 G2
Burniston Cl PL7 27 E5
Burns Av PL5 17 E5
Burraton Rd PL12 14 B3
Burrington Ind Est PL5 16 D5
Burrington Rd PL5 16 D5
Burrington Way PL5 16 D6
Burrow Hill, Bodmin PL31 31 E5
Burrow Hill, Plymouth PL9 30 D4
Burton Cl PL6 12 C6
Burwell Cl PL6 19 E3
Bush Pk PL6 19 F3
Bute Rd PL4 24 A4
Butler Cl PL6 12 B6
Butt Park Rd PL5 17 E4
Butterdon Walk PL21 36 F2
Butterdown PL12 14 B3
Byard Cl PL5 16 B5
Byland Rd PL3 24 B3
Byron Av PL5 17 E4

Cabot Cl PL12 15 E4
Cadleigh Cl PL21 35 C5
Cadleigh La PL21 35 D4
Cadover Cl PL6 18 B5
Caernarvon Gdns PL2 23 E1
Calder Cl PL3 24 C3
Caldicot Gdns PL6 12 C4
Caledonia Cl PL7 27 F3
California Gdns PL3 25 E2
Callington Rd PL12 14 C2
Calstock Rd PL18 6 E2
Calvez Cl PL10 33 C1
Camber Rd PL1 28 D4
Camborne Cl PL5 16 D1
Cambridge Rd PL2 22 C3
Camden St PL4 4 E3
Cameron Dr PL21 36 A3
Cameron Way PL6 18 C6
Camilla Ter PL2 23 G1
Campbell Rd PL31 31 F3
Camperdown St PL2 22 C4
Camperknowle Cl PL10 33 C1
Campion Cl, Plymouth PL7 27 G4
Campion Cl, Saltash PL12 14 D2
Campion Vw PL6 13 E4
Candish Dr PL9 32 B1
Canefields Av PL7 27 F5
Canhaye Cl PL7 27 E5
Cann Gdns PL6 11 C6
Cann Wood Vw PL6 13 E5
Cannon St PL1 28 A2
Canterbury Cl PL21 36 E3
Canterbury Dr PL5 17 E2
Caprera Pl PL4 4 C2
Caprera Ter PL4 4 C2
Captains Gdns PL5 17 G5
Caradon Cl PL6 18 B2
Caradon Ter PL12 15 E3
Carbeile Rd PL11 21 F5
Cardiff Cl PL7 27 F4
Cardigan Rd PL6 18 C6
Cardinal Av PL5 16 B6
Careswell Av PL2 16 C6
Carew Av PL5 17 E4
Carew Gdns, Plymouth PL5 17 E3
Carew Gdns, Saltash PL12 14 C3
Carew Gro PL5 17 E4
Carew Ter PL11 21 H6
Carey Ct PL12 15 E3
Carisbrooke Rd PL6 18 C6
Carlisle Rd PL5 17 F3
Carlton Cl PL3 24 B3
Carlton Ter, Lipson PL4 24 A6
Carlton Ter, Weston Mill PL5 22 B1
Carlyon Cl PL11 21 E5
Carmarthen Rd PL4 24 B6
Carnock Rd PL2 17 G6
Carnoustie Dr PL12 14 C5
Carolina Gdns PL2 22 C1
Caroline Pl PL1 28 D3
Carpenter Rd PL31 31 F3
Carradale Rd PL6 24 D1
Carrisbrooke Way PL12 14 B4
Carroll Rd PL5 17 F4
Carron La PL6 12 D3
Carter Rd PL21 36 D1
Castle Acre Gdns PL3 24 C3
Castle Bank Gdns PL3 24 C3
Castle Cary Gdns PL3 24 C3
Castle Ct PL12 14 B4
Castle Dyke La PL1 5 E6
Castle Hill PL12 14 B6
Castle La PL7 26 C4
Castle Rise, Plymouth PL3 24 C4
Castle Rise, Saltash PL12 14 C5
Castle St PL1 5 E7
Castle Vw PL12 14 C5
Castlehayes Gdns PL7 26 C4
Castlemead Cl PL12 14 D4
Castlemead Dr PL12 14 C4
Castleton Cl PL3 24 A4
Catalina Villas PL9 30 A4
Cathcart Av PL4 30 B1
Cathedral St PL1 29 E2
Catherine St PL1 5 D5
Cattedown Rd PL4 30 A1
Catterick Cl PL5 16 B1
Cattewater Rd PL4 30 B1
Cavendish Rd PL4 30 B1
Caxton Gdns PL5 17 F5
Cayley Way PL5 16 C4
Cecil Av PL4 24 B6
Cecil St PL1 4 A3
Cedar Av PL9 30 C5
Cedar Cl PL11 21 F6
Cedar Ct PL12 15 F4
Cedar Dr PL11 21 E6
Cedarcroft Rd PL2 23 E1
Celandine Gdns PL7 27 G4
Cemetery Rd PL18 6 D4
Central Av PL21 35 B4
Central Park Av PL3 4 B2
Central Rd PL1 5 A7
Central St PL1 29 E3
Chaddlewood Av PL4 24 A6
Chaddlewood Cl PL7 27 E4
Chagford Walk PL6 25 F1
Challgood Cl PL31 31 F5
Challgood Rise PL31 31 E5
Challock Cl PL6 18 D2
Chamberlayne Dr PL7 26 C3
Channel Park Av PL3 24 B3
Channel View Ter PL4 24 B5
Channon Rd PL12 14 C2
Chantry Ct PL7 25 H3
Chapel Cl, Gunnislake PL18 6 B3
Chapel Cl, Yelverton PL20 8 C2
Chapel La PL20 8 C2
Chapel Pl PL21 36 D2
Chapel Rd, Plymouth PL8 35 C2
Chapel Rd, Saltash PL12 14 B3
Chapel Row PL11 21 H6
Chapel St, Devonport PL1 28 B2
Chapel St, Gunnislake PL18 6 E2
Chapel St, Plymouth PL4 4 E4
Chapel St, Yelverton PL20 11 B2
Chapel Street Ope PL1 28 B2
Chapel Way PL3 24 B2
Chapeldown Rd PL11 21 F6
Chapman Ct PL12 14 B3
Chapmans Ope PL1 28 A2
Chard Barton PL5 17 E4
Chard Rd PL5 16 B4
Charfield Dr PL6 18 A6
Charles Hankin Way PL21 36 E3
Charles St PL4 4 D4
Charles Ter PL3 24 B3
Charlescross PL4 4 E4
Charlotte St PL2 22 B4
Charlton Cres PL6 18 B4
Charlton Rd PL6 18 A4
Charlton Ter PL21 36 D2
Charnhill Cl PL31 31 G5
Charnhill Way PL31 31 G5
Chatsworth Gdns PL5 16 C4
Chaucer Way PL5 17 E5
Chawleigh Cl PL18 6 D3
Chedworth St PL4 4 F3
Chelmer Cl PL7 27 E4
Chelmsford Pl PL5 17 F2
Chelson Gdns PL6 19 F4
Cheltenham Pl PL4 4 F1
Chepstow Av PL6 12 C4
Chequers Haigh PL8 34 B6
Cheriton Cl PL5 16 D3
Cherry Pk PL7 27 E5
Cherry Tree Dr PL8 32 E3
Cherry Tree La PL7 27 E5
Cheshire Dr PL6 11 B6
Chester Pl PL4 4 E1
Chesterfield Rd PL3 24 B4
Chesterton Cl PL5 17 F4
Chestnut Av PL9 30 C5
Chestnut Cl, Saltash PL12 14 D2
Chestnut Cl, Torpoint PL11 21 F6
Chestnut Rd PL3 23 G1
Chichester Cres PL12 15 E5
Chichester Ct PL20 8 C2
Childrey Gdns PL6 18 D5
Childrey Walk PL6 18 D6
Chilton Cl PL6 24 B1
Chittleburn Hill PL8 32 C4
Chivenor Av PL5 16 B2
Christian Mill Bsns Pk PL6 17 H3
Chubb Dr PL3 23 E4
Chudleigh Rd PL4 24 B4
Church Cl, Woodford PL7 25 H1
Church Cl, Yealmpton PL8 35 B1
Church Cotts PL8 32 E4
Church Hill, Calstock PL18 7 F6
Church Hill, Plymouth PL6 18 B5
Church Hill Rd PL9 30 A4
Church La, Calstock PL18 7 F7
Church La, Plymouth PL8 35 B2
Church Mdw PL21 36 A3
Church Park Ct PL6 13 F4
Church Park Rd, Newton Ferrers PL8 34 C5
Church Park Rd, Woolwell PL6 13 E4
Church Park Rd, Yealmpton PL8 35 C3
Church Pk, Plymouth PL8 34 C5
Church Pk, Yelverton PL20 8 D3
Church Rd, Bodmin PL31 31 E3
Church Rd, Plympton PL7 26 D4
Church Rd, Saltash PL12 14 D3
Church Rd, Wembury PL9 34 B3
Church Row La PL5 11 B6
Church St, Calstock PL18 7 F7
Church St, Plymouth PL3 22 D4
Church Walk PL9 34 B2
Church Way, St Budeaux PL5 16 B6
Church Way, Yealmpton PL8 35 B2
Churchill Walk PL12 15 E5
Churchill Way PL3 23 H2
Churchlands Cl PL6 13 F5
Churchlands Rd PL6 13 F4
Churchstow Walk PL6 19 E6
Churchtown Vale PL12 14 D5
Churchways PL31 31 H4
Citadel Rd PL1 5 A6
Citadel Rd East PL1 5 D6
Clare Pl PL4 29 H3
Clare St PL21 36 C3
Claremont St PL1 4 B2
Clarence Pl, Morice Town PL2 22 B5
Clarence Pl, Stonehouse PL1 28 D2
Clarence Rd PL11 21 G5
Clarendon La PL2 22 D5
Claymans Pathway PL21 36 A1
Clayton Pl PL4 30 B1
Clayton Rd PL4 30 B1
Clear Vw PL12 15 E3
Clearbrook Av PL5 16 B5
Cleeve Dr PL21 36 B2
Cleeve Gdns PL2 16 D6
Clegg Av PL11 21 E5
Clement Rd PL7 27 F4
Clevedon Park Av PL2 23 E2
Cleveland Rd PL4 24 B6
Cliff Rd, Plymouth PL1 5 A7
Cliff Rd, Wembury PL9 34 A1
Cliff Rd, Wembury PL9 34 B3
Cliff View Ter PL18 6 F2
Clifford Cl PL5 16 B4
Clifton Av PL7 26 C1
Clifton Cl PL7 26 C1
Clifton Pl PL4 4 E2
Clifton St PL4 4 F2
Clinton Av PL4 24 B5
Clinton Ter PL10 33 B1
Clittaford Rd PL6 11 D6
Clittaford Vw PL6 11 D5
Clonway PL20 9 D5
Clovelly Rd PL4 30 A2
Clovelly Vw PL9 30 A4
Clover Rise PL6 13 E5
Clover Walk PL12 14 B3
Clowance Cl PL1 28 B3
Clowance La PL1 28 B3
Clowance St PL1 28 B3
Clyde St PL2 22 C3
Coach House Mews PL31 31 G4
Coach Rd PL8 34 B6
Cobb La PL31 31 F4
Cobbett Rd PL5 17 E5
Cobourg St PL1 4 C3
Cobourgh St PL1 29 F2
Cockington Cl PL6 19 E5

Cockington Walk PL6 18 D6
Colborne Rd PL6 18 B4
Coldrenick St PL5 16 A6
Cole La PL21 36 D1
Colebrook La PL7 26 C2
Colebrook Rd, Plympton PL7 26 C2
Colebrook Rd, St Budeaux PL5 16 B5
Coleman Dr PL31 31 F6
Coleridge Av PL6 17 H5
Coleridge La PL4 18 A3
Coleridge Rd PL4 24 A5
Colesdown Hill, Bodmin PL31 31 F2
Colesdown Hill, Plymouth PL9 25 H6
Colin Campbell Ct PL1 5 A5
Collafield Cl PL7 27 E5
College Av PL4 23 H4
College Dean Cl PL6 18 D1
College La PL4 23 H4
College Park Pl PL3 23 G4
College Rd PL2 22 B4
College Vw PL3 23 G4
Colliers Cl PL9 34 C2
Collin Cl PL5 16 A5
Collingwood Av PL4 30 A1
Collingwood Rd PL1 28 C1
Collingwood Villas PL1 28 C1
Collins Pk PL3 24 A2
Colne Gdns PL3 24 C3
Colston Cl PL6 12 C6
Coltishall Cl PL5 16 C2
Coltness Rd PL31 31 G5
Coltsfield Cl PL6 18 C6
Colville Walk PL1 28 A1
Colwill Rd PL6 19 F3
Colwill Walk PL6 19 F3
Colwyn Rd PL11 21 G6
Combley Dr PL6 19 E2
Commercial Ope PL4 29 H4
Commercial Rd, Calstock PL18 7 F7
Commercial Rd, Plymouth PL4 29 H3
Commercial Rd, Yelverton PL20 8 D2
Commercial St, Gunnislake PL18 6 E1
Commercial St, Plymouth PL4 29 H4
Compass Dr PL7 27 E1
Compton Av PL3 24 A3
Compton Knoll Cl PL3 24 B2
Compton Leigh PL3 24 A2
Compton Park Rd PL3 24 A3
Compton Vale PL3 24 B3
Congreve Gdns PL5 17 F5
Coniston Gdns PL6 18 A2
Connaught Av PL4 23 H4
Connaught La PL4 23 H4
Conqueror Dr PL5 17 H5
Conrad Rd PL5 17 F5
Consort Cl PL3 23 H2
Constable Cl PL5 17 G4
Constantine St PL4 4 E4
Convent Cl PL12 15 E3
Conway Gdns PL2 23 E1
Conyngham Ct PL6 18 A6
Cooban Ct PL6 18 A6
Cook Ct PL12 14 B3
Cookworthy Rd PL2 22 C2
Coombe Down La PL8 34 B6
Coombe La PL6 11 B6
Coombe Park Cl PL10 33 C5
Coombe Park La PL5 16 D3
Coombe Pk, Saltash PL12 15 F5
Coombe Pk, Torpoint PL10 33 C5
Coombe PL12 15 F5
Coombe Way PL5 17 G1
Copleston Rd PL6 17 G1
Coppard Mdws PL7 26 A2
Copper Beech Way PL6 12 D5
Coppers Pk PL6 13 E5
Coppice Gdns PL5 17 G4
Coppice Wood Dr PL6 12 D5
Copse Cl PL7 26 B4
Copse Rd PL7 26 B4
Copthorne Gdns PL31 31 F5
Corea Ter PL1 28 C2
Corfe Av PL3 24 A1
Corfe Cl PL21 36 D3
Coringdean Cl PL6 12 C6

Corner Brake PL6 13 E5
Cornfield Gdns PL7 27 F1
Cornwall Beach PL1 28 A2
Cornwall St, Devonport PL1 28 A2
Cornwall St, Plymouth PL1 4 B4
Cornwall St, Yelverton PL20 11 B2
Cornwood Rd, Ivybridge PL21 36 A2
Cornwood Rd, Plymouth PL7 27 F4
Cornworthy Cl PL2 22 D1
Coronation Cotts PL11 21 G6
Coronation Pl PL5 16 B6
Corondale Rd PL2 23 E1
Corporation Rd PL2 23 G1
Corsham Cl PL6 12 C6
Cory Ct PL9 34 D1
Cosdon Pl PL6 18 A5
Costly St PL21 36 D2
Cot Hill PL7 25 H3
Cot Hill Cl PL7 25 H3
Cot Hill Dr PL7 25 H3
Cotehele Av, Keyham PL2 22 C3
Cotehele Av, Prince Rock PL4 30 A1
Cothele Vw PL18 7 E7
Cottage Grn PL8 34 C5
Cottage Mews PL7 26 C4
Cotton Cl PL7 26 D4
County Cl PL7 27 E3
Court Rd PL8 34 A5
Court Vw PL8 32 D4
Court Wood PL8 34 A5
Courtenay St PL1 5 B5
Courtfield Rd PL3 24 A3
Courtland Cres PL7 26 B2
Courtlands PL12 14 D5
Cove Mdw PL11 21 F2
Coverdale Pl PL5 17 E5
Cowdray Cl PL12 15 E4
Cowdray Ter PL12 14 D5
Cowley Rd PL5 17 G4
Cox Tor Cl PL20 9 D6
Coxs Cl PL6 18 C6
Coypool Rd PL7 25 G2
Crabtree Cl PL3 25 F3
Crabtree Villas PL3 25 F3
Crackston Cl PL6 24 B1
Craigie Dr PL1 28 D2
Craigmore Av PL2 22 C4
Cramber Cl PL6 12 D3
Cranbourne Av PL4 24 A6
Cranfield PL7 26 A1
Cranmere Rd PL3 24 B2
Crantock Ter PL2 22 D3
Crapstone Rd PL20 9 C6
Crashaw Cl PL5 17 G4
Craven Av PL4 24 B6
Crawford Rd PL1 28 D1
Creamery Cl PL8 35 C2
Crediton Walk PL6 25 F1
Creedy Rd PL3 24 C3
Cremyll Rd PL11 21 G6
Cremyll St PL1 28 D3
Crescent Av PL1 5 A6
Crescent Avenue Mews PL1 5 B6
Crescent Gdns PL21 36 C2
Crescent Rd PL21 36 C2
Cressbrook Cl PL6 19 F4
Cressbrook Dr PL6 19 F4
Cressbrook Walk PL6 19 F4
Crestfield Rise PL21 36 A3
Cresthill Rd PL2 23 E1
Crockers Row PL18 6 F2
Croft Pk PL6 12 D5
Cromartie Rd PL4 30 B1
Cromer Cl PL6 12 A5
Cromer Walk PL6 12 A5
Cromwell Gate PL6 12 D5
Cromwell Rd PL4 30 A1
Crookeder Cl PL31 31 G5
Cross Hill PL2 22 B4
Cross Park Av PL6 17 H5
Cross Park Rd, Manadon PL6 17 H5
Cross Park Rd, Plympton PL9 34 C2
Cross Park Way PL6 18 A5
Cross Pk PL8 32 E4
Crossway PL7 26 B1
Crossway Av PL4 24 C5
Crossways PL9 34 C2
Crow La PL18 6 C3
Crow Pk PL3 24 A4

Crowndale Av PL3 24 B2
Crownhill Fort Rd PL6 17 H4
Crownhill Rd PL5 16 C3
Croydon Gdns PL5 16 B2
Crozier Rd PL4 24 A4
Cuffe Rd PL3 23 F4
Culbin Grn PL6 24 D1
Culdrose Cl PL5 16 B3
Culme Rd PL3 24 A4
Culver Cl PL6 18 A6
Culver Rd PL12 15 F4
Culver Way PL6 24 D1
Culverwood Cl PL7 27 G3
Cumberland Rd PL1 28 B3
Cumberland St PL1 28 B3
Cundy Cl PL7 25 H1
Cunliffe Av PL9 34 D1
Cunningham Rd PL5 11 B4
Curlew Cl PL10 33 C1
Curlew Mews PL3 24 A4
Cursons Way PL21 36 A2
Curtis St PL1 28 B3
Custom House La PL1 29 E4
Cypress Cl PL7 27 G3

Dairy La PL21 36 D2
Dale Av PL6 24 C1
Dale Gdns PL4 4 C1
Dale Rd PL4 4 C1
Dalton Gdns PL5 16 C4
Damerel Cl PL1 28 C3
Danum Dr PL7 27 F5
Dark Street La PL7 26 C4
Darklake Cl PL6 19 F1
Darklake La PL6 13 E4
Darklake Vw PL6 19 E1
Dart Cl PL3 25 E2
Dartington Walk PL6 19 E6
Dartmeet Av PL3 24 C2
Dartmoor Vw, Plymouth PL4 24 C5
Dartmoor Vw, Saltash PL12 14 D2
Dartmouth Walk PL6 19 E6
Darwin Cres PL3 25 E4
Davenham Cl PL6 12 B6
David Cl PL7 26 D2
Davy Cl PL11 21 E5
Davy Rd PL6 18 D3
Dawes La, Plymouth PL9 32 A2
Dawes La, Torpoint PL10 33 B2
Dawlish Walk PL6 25 E1
Daws Ct PL5 15 F4
Dawson Cl PL5 16 B5
Daymond Rd PL6 16 A4
Dayton Cl PL6 17 H4
De La Hay Av PL3 23 E5
De La Hay Villas PL3 23 E5
Deacon Cl PL5 15 F5
Deacon Dr PL12 15 E5
Dean Cross Rd PL31 31 E3
Dean Hill PL31 31 E3
Dean Park Rd PL9 30 D4
Dean Rd PL7 26 B2
Debden Cl PL7 16 B2
Deeble Cl PL7 26 C1
Deep La PL7 27 G5
Deer Park Dr PL3 24 D2
Deer Pk, Ivybridge PL21 36 E3
Deer Pk, Saltash PL12 15 E3
Defoe Cl PL5 17 F5
Delacombe Cl PL7 26 D1
Delamere Cl PL6 24 D1
Delamere Ct PL21 36 A3
Delaware Ct PL18 6 D3
Delaware Gdns PL2 22 C1
Delaware Rd PL18 6 C1
Delgany Dr PL6 18 B2
Delgany Villas PL6 18 B1
Delgany Vw PL6 18 B1
Dengie Cl PL7 27 F3
Denham Cl PL5 17 F4
Dennis Cl PL5 21 H1
Deptford Pl PL4 4 E2
Derby Rd PL5 17 F3
Derriford Bsns Pk PL6 18 B3
Derriford Pk PL6 18 B3
Derriford Rd PL6 18 B2
Derry Av PL4 4 D1
Derrys Cross PL1 5 B5
Derwent Av PL3 24 C4
Desborough La PL4 30 A1
Desborough Rd PL4 30 A1
Deveron Cl PL7 27 E4
Devon Ter PL3 23 G4
Devon Tors Rd PL20 9 E6

Devonia Cl PL7 26 C1
Devonport Hill, Plymouth PL1 28 C3
Devonport Hill, Torpoint PL10 33 D5
Devonport Rd PL1 28 C2
Devonshire St PL4 4 F3
Diamond Av PL4 24 A5
Dickens Rd PL5 17 E5
Dickiemoor La PL5 17 F4
Dieppe Cl PL1 28 B2
Digby Gro PL5 16 C1
Dillons PL8 34 C5
Dingle Rd, North Prospect PL2 22 D2
Dingle Rd, Plympton PL7 26 A3
Dingwall Av PL5 17 H3
Dirty La PL12 14 B1
Distine Cl PL3 24 C2
Dittisham Walk PL6 25 F1
Ditton Ct PL6 18 A6
Dixon Pl PL2 22 C4
Dixon Ter PL8 35 B2
Dockray Cl PL6 18 D3
Doddridge Cl PL31 31 F6
Doidges Farm Cl PL6 18 C6
Dolphin Cl PL31 31 F4
Dolphin Court Rd PL31 31 F4
Dolphin Sq PL31 31 F4
Donkey La PL21 36 C2
Donnington Dr PL3 24 C2
Dorchester Av PL5 17 G3
Doreena Rd PL9 32 A2
Dormy Av PL3 24 A3
Dorsmouth Ter PL7 26 C4
Douglas St PL2 24 D3
Douglass Rd PL3 24 D3
Douro Ct PL21 36 D2
Dousland Rd PL20 9 E6
Dove Gdns PL3 24 D2
Dovedale Rd PL2 22 D1
Dover Rd PL6 19 E3
Down Cl PL12 14 C5
Down Rd PL7 27 F3
Downfield Dr PL7 26 D3
Downfield Walk PL7 27 E3
Downfield Way PL7 26 D3
Downgate Gdns PL2 17 G6
Downham Gdns PL5 11 B5
Downhorne Pk PL31 31 E4
Downside Av PL6 24 C1
Downton Cl PL1 29 E2
Drake Circus PL4 4 D3
Drake Ct PL4 24 A6
Drake Way PL31 31 E4
Drakefield Dr PL12 15 F3
Drakes Pl PL6 18 A2
Drakewalls Gdns PL18 6 D3
Drax Gdns PL3 17 H6
Drayton Rd PL5 17 F5
Drovers Way PL21 36 A1
Drummond Cl PL2 22 C1
Drummond Pl PL1 28 B1
Drunken Bridge Hill PL7 26 A5
Dryburgh Cres PL2 22 D1
Dryden Av PL5 17 F5
Ducane Walk PL6 18 B5
Duckworth St PL2 22 D4
Dudley Gdns PL6 18 C6
Dudley Rd PL7 25 H3
Duke St PL1 28 B3
Duloe Gdns PL2 17 F6
Dumfries Av PL5 17 G3
Duncan St PL1 28 B3
Dunclair Pk PL3 25 E4
Duncombe Av PL5 16 D4
Dundas St PL2 22 D4
Dundonald St PL2 22 C4
Dunheved Rd PL12 15 E4
Dunkeswell Cl PL6 12 D6
Dunley Walk PL6 18 D6
Dunnet Rd PL6 11 C6
Dunraven Dr PL6 18 A1
Dunstan Cl PL7 27 G4
Dunstone Av PL31 31 F4
Dunstone Cl PL31 31 F4
Dunstone Dr PL31 31 F3
Dunstone La PL31 31 G4
Dunstone Rd, Bodmin PL31 31 F4
Dunstone Rd, Plymouth PL5 16 C3
Dunstone Vw PL31 31 F3
Durban Rd PL3 23 G3
Durham Av PL4 24 B5
Durnford St PL1 28 D3

Durnford Street Ope PL1 28 C4
Durrant Cl PL1 28 B2
Durris Cl PL6 19 E2
Durris Gdns PL6 19 E2
Durwent Cl PL9 30 A4
Duxford Cl PL5 16 B2
Dynevor Cl PL3 24 A1

Eagle Rd PL7 27 G4
Earls Acre PL3 23 F5
Earls Dr PL10 33 D5
Earls Mill Rd PL7 26 C3
Earls Wood Dr PL6 19 F3
Earlswood Cl PL6 19 G3
East Park Av PL4 4 C1
East St PL1 28 D3
East Way PL21 35 C5
Eastbury Av PL5 16 D4
Eastcote Cl PL6 12 C6
Eastella Rd PL20 9 F6
Easterdown Cl PL31 31 F3
Eastern Wood Rd PL7 27 H3
Eastfield Av PL9 30 C5
Eastlake St PL1 4 D4
Eastlake Walk PL1 4 D4
Ebrington St PL4 4 E4
Ebrington Street Ope PL1 4 D4
Eddystone Cl PL3 24 D2
Eddystone Ter PL1 5 A8
Eden Cotts PL21 36 D2
Edenside PL3 23 H2
Edgar Ter PL4 24 A4
Edgcumbe Av PL1 28 D2
Edgcumbe Cres PL10 33 C1
Edgcumbe Park Rd PL3 23 G2
Edgcumbe Rd PL12 14 C1
Edgcumbe St PL1 28 D3
Edgecombe Way PL18 6 A4
Edinburgh St PL1 28 A3
Edith Av PL4 24 B5
Edith St PL5 16 A5
Edna Ter PL4 24 B6
Edwards Cl PL7 27 F4
Edwards Cres PL12 14 B4
Edwards Dr PL7 27 F4
Effingham Cres PL3 23 G1
Efford Cres PL3 24 C2
Efford Pathway PL3 24 C2
Efford Rd PL3 24 B2
Efford Walk PL3 24 B3
Egerton Cres PL4 24 B6
Egerton Pl PL4 24 A6
Egerton Rd PL4 24 A6
Eggbuckland Rd PL3,6 24 B2
Egret Cl PL10 33 C1
Eight Acres Cl PL7 27 G3
Elaine Cl PL7 26 A4
Elan Cl PL5 17 G4
Elbridge Cotts PL8 32 E4
Elburton Rd, Bodmin PL31 31 F2
Elburton Rd, Plymouth PL9 32 A2
Eldad Hill PL1 28 D2
Elder Cl PL7 27 F3
Elford Cres PL7 26 C1
Elford Dr PL9 30 C3
Elford PL20 9 E6
Elford Town PL20 9 E7
Elgin Cres PL5 17 H4
Elim Ct PL3 23 H3
Elim Ter PL3 23 H3
Elinor Pl PL4 24 A5
Eliot Gdns PL4 30 B1
Eliot St PL5 16 B6
Elizabeth Cl PL21 36 F2
Elizabeth Pl PL4 4 D2
Elliot Sq PL11 21 H6
Elliot St PL1 5 B7
Elliot Ter PL1 5 B7
Elliot Terrace La PL1 5 B7
Elliott Cl PL12 14 D4
Elliott Rd PL4 30 A1
Elliotts Hill PL8 32 E4
Ellwell Rd PL12 15 F4
Elm Cres PL3 24 A4
Elm Croft PL6 19 E1
Elm Gro, Eggbuckland PL6 18 C6
Elm Gro, Plympton PL7 26 C3
Elm Rd PL4 24 A4
Elm Ter PL4 24 A4
Elm Tree Cl PL8 35 B1

Elm Tree Pk PL8 35 B1
Elmcroft PL2 23 E2
Elmwood Cl PL6 18 D1
Elphinstone Rd PL4 23 F2
Elwick Gdns PL3 24 C3
Embankment La PL4 30 B1
Embankment Rd PL4 30 A1
Emily Gdns PL4 24 A5
Emma Pl PL1 28 C3
Emma Place Ope PL1 28 D3
Endsleigh Gdns PL4 4 D2
Endsleigh Park Rd PL3 23 G2
Endsleigh Rd PL4 4 D2
Endsleigh Rd PL9 30 C3
Endsleigh Vw PL21 36 A3
Ennerdale Cres PL6 17 H2
Epping Cres PL6 24 D1
Epworth Ter PL2 22 C3
Eric Rd PL4 30 A1
Erith Av PL2 22 C1
Erle Gdns PL7 26 D5
Erlstoke Cl PL6 18 D5
Erme Ct PL21 36 D3
Erme Dr PL21 36 C2
Erme Gdns PL3 24 D3
Erme Mews PL21 36 C3
Erme Rd PL21 36 D2
Ermington Ter PL4 4 E1
Ernesettle Cres PL5 16 B3
Ernesettle Grn PL5 16 B2
Ernesettle La PL5 16 A1
Ernesettle Rd PL5 16 B4
Esmonde Gdns PL5 15 H6
Essa Rd PL12 15 E4
Essex St PL1 4 A3
Esso Wharf Rd PL4 30 A3
Estover Cl PL6 19 F2
Estover Ind Est PL6 19 F2
Estover Rd PL6 19 F2
Eton Av PL1 4 B3
Eton Pl PL1 4 B3
Eton St PL1 4 B3
Eton Ter PL1 4 B3
Evans Pl PL2 23 E3
Evelyn Pl PL4 4 E1
Evelyn St PL5 16 A5
Evenden Ct PL11 21 F5
Exchange St PL4 5 E6
Exe Gdns PL3 24 D2
Exeter Rd PL21 36 D2
Exeter St PL4 4 E4
Exmouth Rd PL1 28 B1

Fairfax Ter PL2 22 C4
Fairfield PL7 26 C2
Fairfield Av PL2 23 F1
Fairmead Mews PL4 14 C4
Fairmead Rd PL12 14 C3
Fairview Av PL3 25 E4
Fairview Way PL3 25 E3
Fairway PL12 14 C5
Fairway Av PL12 36 B2
Fanshawe Way PL9 30 C5
Faraday Mill Bsns Pk PL4 30 B2
Faraday Rd PL4 30 B1
Farm Cl PL7 26 A2
Farm La, Plymouth PL5 17 E4
Farm La, Saltash PL12 14 D5
Farnley Cl PL6 12 B6
Farringdon Rd PL4 24 B5
Fayre Vw PL12 14 A6
Fearnside Way PL12 14 C3
Federation Rd PL3 24 D4
Fegan Rd PL5 15 G6
Fellowes Pl PL1 28 D2
Fenten Pk PL12 15 E4
Fern Cl PL7 27 F3
Fernbank Av PL21 36 A1
Ferndale Av PL2 22 B1
Ferndale Cl PL6 12 D5
Ferndale Rd PL2 22 B1
Fernhill Cl PL21 36 B2
Fernleigh Rd PL3 24 A4
Ferrers Rd PL5 16 B5
Ferry La PL11 20 C2
Ferry Rd PL1 28 A1
Ferry St PL11 21 H6
Feversham Cl PL7 27 E3
Filham Moor Cl PL21 36 E3
Fillace La PL20 8 C2
Fillace Pk PL20 8 D3
Filham Moor La PL21 36 D2
Fincer Dr PL21 36 A2
Finch Cl PL3 24 D4
Finches Cl PL9 32 A2
Findon Gdns PL6 18 D2

Finewell St PL1 5 D5
Finnigan Rd PL4 30 B2
Fircroft Rd PL2 23 E1
First Av, Bodmin PL31 31 F2
First Av, Plymouth PL1 28 C2
Firtree Rd PL6 19 E1
Firtree Rise PL21 36 D2
Fisgard Way PL11 19 D5
Fisher Rd PL2 22 D3
Fistral Cl PL11 21 E5
Fitzroy Rd PL1 28 C2
Fitzroy Ter PL1 28 D1
Flamborough Rd PL6 12 B5
Flamborough Way PL6 12 B6
Flamsteed Cres PL5 16 C5
Fleet St PL2 22 B2
Fletcher Cres PL31 31 G4
Fletcher Way PL31 31 G4
Fletemoor Rd PL5 16 A6
Flora Cotts PL1 5 A5
Flora Ct PL1 4 A4
Flora St PL1 5 A5
Florence Pl PL4 30 A1
Florence St PL5 16 A5
Floyd Cl PL2 22 D1
Foliot Av PL2 22 D2
Foliot Rd PL2 22 C1
Ford Cl PL21 36 A2
Ford Hill PL2 22 D4
Ford Park La PL4 23 H4
Ford Park Rd PL4 23 G4
Ford Pk PL4 23 H4
Ford Rd, Wembury PL9 34 A1
Ford Rd, Yealmpton PL8 35 B2
Forder Heights PL6 18 C5
Forder Hill PL10 33 B6
Forder La PL10 33 C6
Forder Valley Rd PL6 18 B4
Fore St, Cawsand PL10 33 D5
Fore St, Devonport PL1 28 B2
Fore St, Drakewalls PL18 6 C4
Fore St, Gunnislake PL18 6 E2
Fore St, Ivybridge PL21 36 C3
Fore St, Millbrook PL10 33 B2
Fore St, Plympton PL7 26 C4
Fore St, Saltash PL12 15 F4
Fore St, Tamerton Foliot PL5 11 A6
Fore St, Torpoint PL11 21 H5
Fore St, Yealmpton PL8 35 B1
Fore St, Yelverton PL20 11 C2
Forest Av PL2 23 F1
Forest Vw PL6 13 E5
Foresters Rd PL9 30 D3
Forge Cl PL6 12 D3
Forge La PL12 14 C2
Forge Sq PL1 28 B3
Forresters Dr PL6 12 D5
Forster Cl PL7 27 F4
Forsythia Dr PL12 14 B3
Fort Austin Av PL6 18 C5
Fort Ter PL5,6 17 H3
Fortescue Pl PL3 25 E2
Forth Gdns PL3 25 E2
Fosbrooke Ct PL3 24 A3
Foulston Av PL4 15 G6
Foundry La PL8 34 B6
Fountains Cres PL2 17 E6
Fox Ct PL21 36 D3
Fox Field Cl PL3 24 D4
Foxglove Way PL12 14 B3
Foxtor Cl PL5 17 E3
Foxwood Gdns, Bodmin PL31 31 E5
Foxwood Gdns, Plymouth PL6 17 H1
Foyle Cl PL7 27 E4
Francis Pl PL1 29 E2
Francis St PL1 29 E2
Frankfort Gate PL1 4 A4
Franklyns PL6 18 B2
Franklyns Cl PL6 18 B2
Fraser Pl PL5 11 B5
Fraser Rd PL5 11 B5
Fraser Sq PL5 11 B5
Frederick St East PL1 29 E2

Frederick St West PL1 29 E2
Fredington Gro PL2 23 E3
Freemans Wharf PL1 28 D4
Freemantle Gdns PL2 22 C4
Freemantle Pl PL2 22 C4
Frensham Av PL6 12 D6
Frensham Gdns PL6 12 C5
Freshford Cl PL6 18 D5
Freshford Walk PL6 18 D5
Frewin Gdns PL6 12 B6
Friars La PL1 5 D6

Friary Pk Trading Est PL4

Frith Rd PL12 14 D3
Frobisher App PL5 17 G4
Frobisher Dr PL12 15 E5
Frobisher Way PL11 19 D5
Frogmore Av PL6 24 C1
Frogmore Ct PL6 24 C1
Frome Cl PL7 27 E4
Frontfield Cres PL6 17 G1
Fullerton Rd PL2 22 D4
Furland Cl PL9 30 C5
Furneaux Av PL2 23 E3
Furneaux Rd PL2 23 E3
Fursdon Cl PL31 31 H4
Furse Pk PL5 21 H1
Furzeacre Cl PL7 27 E2
Furzehatt Av PL31 31 G5
Furzehatt Park Rd PL31 31 G4
Furzehatt Rd PL31 31 G4
Furzehatt Rise PL31 31 G4
Furzehatt Villas PL31 31 F5
Furzehatt Way PL31 31 G5
Furzehill Rd PL4 4 F1

Galileo Cl PL7 26 C2
Gallacher Way PL12 14 B3
Galsworthy Cl PL5 17 F4
Galva Rd PL7 27 G1
Ganges Rd PL2 22 D3
Ganna Park Rd PL3 23 G3
Gara Cl PL31 31 H5
Garden Cl PL1 27 H4
Garden Cres PL1 5 A7
Garden Park Cl PL31 31 H4
Garden St PL2 22 B5
Garden Village PL31 31 F2
Gards La PL5 16 B5
Garfield Ter PL1 28 C1
Garrett St PL10 33 D6
Garrick Cl PL5 17 F4
Garrison Cl PL1 28 B4
Garston Cl PL31 31 G3
Gas House La PL18 6 F2
Gascoyne Pl PL4 4 F4
Gashouse La PL4 29 H3
Gasking St PL4 5 F5
Gdynia Way PL4 30 A1
Geasons La PL7 26 C3
Gennys Cl PL18 6 A3
George Av PL7 26 D4
George La PL7 26 D4
George Pl PL1 28 B3
George St PL1 28 B3
Gibbon La PL4 4 E4
Gibbon St PL4 4 E4
Gifford Pl PL3 23 G4
Gifford Terrace Rd PL3 23 G4
Gilbert Ct PL7 27 F3
Gill Pk PL3 24 A3
Gillard Way PL21 35 C4
Gilston Rd PL12 14 C2
Gilwell Av PL31 31 G3
Gilwell Pl PL4 4 E3
Gilwell St PL4 4 E3
Glade Cl PL6 18 B2
Glanville St PL4 4 D3
Glanville Ter PL12 15 F3
Glanvilles Rd PL21 36 D3
Glebe Av PL12 15 E4
Glen Park Av PL4 4 C2
Glen Rd, Mannamead PL3 24 A4
Glen Rd, Plympton PL7 26 B3
Glenavon Rd PL3 23 H3
Glenburn Cl PL3 23 H1
Glendower Rd PL3 23 G4
Gleneagle Av PL3 24 A3
Gleneagle Rd PL3 24 A3
Glenfield Cl PL6 18 D1
Glenfield Rd PL6 18 D1
Glenfield Way PL6 13 E6
Glenhaven Cl PL7 27 G3
Glenholt Cl PL6 13 E6
Glenholt Rd PL6 12 D6
Glenhurst Rd PL3 23 H3

Glenmore Av PL2 22 C4
Glenside Rise PL7 26 C2
Glentor Rd PL3 23 G1
Glenwood Rd PL3 23 H3
Gloucester Ct PL1 4 C3
Goad Av, Plymouth PL4 30 B1
Goad Av, Torpoint PL11 20 D5
Goad Cl PL11 21 E6
Goad Ct PL11 21 E5
Godding Gdns PL6 11 C6
Godwell La PL21 36 E3
Golden Sq PL7 26 C2
Goldfinch Gro PL12 14 D2
Goldsmith Gdns PL5 17 G4
Goodeve Cl PL31 31 E5
Goodin Av PL6 12 A6
Goodwin Cres PL2 22 D2
Gooseberry La PL1 5 A6
Goosewell Hill PL6 18 C6
Goosewell Park Rd PL31 31 F5
Goosewell Rd PL31 31 F5
Goosewell Ter PL31 31 F5
Gordon Ct PL12 14 D4
Gordon Ter, Plymouth PL4 4 D1
Gordon Ter, Torpoint PL11 21 G6
Gorse Way PL21 36 D3
Gorsey Cl PL5 17 H4
Goshen St PL2 22 B3
Goswela Cl PL31 31 D6
Goswela Gdns PL31 31 D6
Gower Ridge Rd PL9 30 D4
Grafton Rd PL4 23 H4
Grainge Rd PL6 18 A6
Granby Ct PL1 28 B2
Granby Grn PL1 28 B2
Granby Pl PL1 28 B2
Granby St PL1 28 B2
Granby Way PL1 28 B2
Grand Hotel Rd PL1 5 B7
Grand Par PL1 5 A8
Grange Rd, Plymouth PL7 26 D4
Grange Rd, Yelverton PL20 9 D5
Grantham Ct PL7 25 H4
Grantley Gdns PL3 24 B4
Grasmere Cl PL6 17 H1
Grassendale Av PL2 22 C1
Grassmere Way PL12 14 D2
Gratton Cl PL7 9 F7
Gratton Pl PL6 18 B6
Gravesend Gdns PL11 21 H5
Gravesend Walk PL11 16 A2
Gray Cres PL5 21 H1
Graybridge Rd PL20 8 C3
Great Berry Rd PL6 17 H5
Great Churchway PL31 31 G4
Great Mis Tor Cl PL20 9 D5
Great Orchard Cl PL31 31 E6
Great Park Cl PL7 27 G3
Great Western Rd PL1 5 A7
Great Woodford Dr PL7 25 H3
Greatfield Rd PL3 24 B2
Greatlands Cres PL2 22 D3
Greatlands Pl PL2 22 D3
Grebe Cl PL7 26 D3
Green La PL20 9 C8
Green Park Av PL4 4 C1
Green Park Rd, Bodmin PL31 31 E5
Green Park Rd, Plymouth PL9 30 D5
Green Pk PL10 33 C5
Green St PL4 4 E4
Greenacres PL31 31 F2
Greenbank Av PL4 24 A6
Greenbank Rd PL4 4 F1
Greenbank Ter, Plymouth PL4 24 A5
Greenbank Ter, Yelverton PL20 9 E6
Greendale Rd PL2 22 D1
Greenfield Dr PL21 36 D3
Greenfield Rd PL12 14 C4
Greenfinch Cres PL31 31 F5
Greenhill Cl PL31 31 F5
Greenland PL10 33 B2
Greenlees Dr PL7 27 F5
Greenway Av PL7 25 H2
Greenway Cl, Ivybridge PL21 36 D3

Greenway Cl, Yelverton PL20 8 C2
Greenwood Cl PL21 36 C3
Greenwood Park Cl PL7 27 F2
Greenwood Park Rd PL7 27 E2
Grenfell Av PL12 14 C3
Grenfell Gdns PL12 14 C3
Grenville Ct PL7 27 F3
Grenville Pk PL20 9 E6
Grenville Rd PL4 4 F4
Gresham Cl PL5 11 B5
Greystoke Av PL6 24 D1
Griffin Way PL31 31 H4
Griggs Cl PL7 27 F5
Grimspound Cl PL6 19 F6
Grimstone Villas PL4 4 D1
Grizedale Rd PL6 25 E1
Grosvenor Rd PL6 18 A4
Grove Pk PL11 21 E5
Guildford Cl PL5 17 H3
Guildford St PL4 4 F3
Gurnard Walk PL3 24 D3
Gurney Cl PL11 21 F5
Guy Miles Way PL5 17 E4

Gwell-Avon Bsns Pk PL12 14 C2
Gwithian Cl PL11 21 E5
Gwyn Rd PL4 24 B5

Haddington Rd PL2 22 C5
Halcyon Ct PL2 22 D2
Halcyon Rd PL2 22 D2
Haldon Pl PL5 16 D3
Hallerton Cl PL6 19 F5
Hallett Cl PL12 14 B3
Halley Gdns PL5 16 C5
Ham Cl PL2 23 E1
Ham Dr PL2 22 D1
Ham Green Ct PL2 22 D1
Ham Green La PL2 23 E1
Ham Grn PL2 22 D1
Ham La PL2 16 C6
Hamble Cl PL3 24 D2
Hamilton Gdns PL4 4 C1
Hamoaze Av PL5 22 B1
Hamoaze Ct PL1 28 B4
Hamoaze Pl PL1 28 A2
Hamoaze Rd PL11 21 G6
Hampton St PL4 4 E4
Hancock Cl PL6 11 C6
Hanover Cl PL3 24 C4
Hanover Rd PL3 24 C4
Harbour Av, Camels Head PL5 22 B1
Harbour Av, Plymouth PL4 5 F5
Harbour St PL11 21 H5
Harbour Vw, Plymouth PL9 30 A4
Harbour Vw, Saltash PL12 15 E4
Hardings Cl PL12 14 D3
Hardy Cres PL5 17 H6
Harebell Cl PL12 14 C2
Hareston Cl PL7 27 F5
Harewood Cl PL7 26 C3
Harewood Cres PL5 16 D4
Harewood Rd PL18 7 F8
Harford Rd PL21 36 D2
Hargood Ter PL2 22 C4
Hargreaves Cl PL6 16 C4
Harlech Cl PL3 24 A1
Harnorlen Rd PL2 23 G1
Haroldsleigh Av PL5 17 H4
Harriet Gdns PL7 26 A2
Harris Ct PL9 30 B5
Harris Way PL21 35 A5
Harrison St PL2 22 C4
Harrowbeer La PL20 9 D5
Hartford St PL2 22 B1
Hartland Cl PL6 12 B5
Hartley Av PL3 24 A2
Hartley Ct, Ivybridge PL21 36 C2
Hartley Ct, Plymouth PL3 24 A2
Hartley Park Gdns PL3 24 A2
Hartley Rd PL3 23 H2
Hartwell Av PL3 32 B2
Harvey St PL11 21 H5
Harwell St PL1 4 A4
Harwell St PL1 4 A4
Harwood Av PL5 11 B5
Hastings St PL1 4 A3
Hastings Ter PL1 4 A3
Haswell Cl PL6 18 A6

Hat La PL10 33 B6
Hatshill Cl PL6 19 G4
Hatshill Farm Cl PL6 13 G3
Havelock Ter PL2 22 C5
Haweswater Cl PL6 17 H2
Hawkers Av PL4 5 F5
Hawkers La PL3 23 H3
Hawkinge Gdns PL5 16 B2
Hawkins Cl PL6 18 B2
Hawks Pk PL12 14 A4
Hawthorn Av PL11 21 F6
Hawthorn Cl,
 Hooe PL9 30 C5
Hawthorn Cl,
 Woolwell PL6 12 D5
Hawthorn Dr PL9 34 C3
Hawthorn Gro PL2 23 F1
Hawthorn Park Rd
 PL9 34 B3
Hawthorn Way PL3 24 C1
Hawthorns PL12 14 D4
Haxter Cl PL6 12 C3
Haydon Gro PL5 15 H6
Haye Rd,
 Bodmin PL31 31 H1
Haye Rd,
 Plymouth PL9 26 A6
Haye Rd South PL31 31 H4
Hayes Pl PL6 18 C6
Hayes Rd PL9 30 C3
Haystone Pl PL1 4 A3
Haytor Cl PL5 17 E3
Haytor Dr PL21 36 D3
Hazel Cl PL6 12 B6
Hazel Dr PL9 32 A2
Hazel Gro,
 Plymouth PL9 32 A1
Hazel Gro,
 Yelverton PL20 9 E6
Hazelwood Cres PL9 32 B2
Hazelwood Dr PL6 12 D5
Headland Pk PL4 4 E1
Healy Pl PL2 22 B5
Heanton Ter PL10 33 B1
Hearl Rd PL12 14 B3
Hearn La PL8 35 H1
Heather Walk PL21 36 D3
Heathfield Pk PL20 9 F5
Heathfield Rd PL4 24 C6
Heavitree Rd PL10 33 D5
Hedgerow Cl PL6 13 F4
Hedingham Cl PL7 27 F4
Hedingham Gdns
 PL6 12 C5
Hele Cl PL6 13 G3
Hele Gdns PL7 26 D4
Hele La PL6 13 G3
Heles Ter PL4 30 B1
Hemerdon Heights
 PL7 27 E2
Hemerdon La PL7 27 G1
Hemerdon Way PL7 26 B2
Henderson Pl PL2 22 C3
Hendwell Cl PL6 11 D6
Henlake Cl PL21 36 B2
Henley Dr PL5 11 B5
Henry Cl PL21 35 A5
Hensbury La PL20 10 D1
Herbert Pl PL2 22 B4
Herbert St PL2 22 B4
Hereford Rd PL5 17 E1
Heritage Cl PL12 14 C3
Hermitage Rd PL3 23 H4
Heron Cl PL10 33 C1
Herschel Gdns PL5 16 B5
Hertland Walk PL2 22 D1
Hessary Dr PL6 12 C1
Hessary Vw PL12 15 E3
Hetling Cl PL1 4 A3
Hewers Row PL4 4 E4
Hewitt Cl PL12 14 C5
Hexham Pl PL2 16 D6
Hexton Hill Rd PL9 30 B5
Heybrook Av PL5 16 B6
Hibernia Ter PL5 22 B1
Hickory Dr PL7 27 F3
Hicks La PL4 5 E5
High Acre Dr PL21 36 A2
High Rd PL9 34 A2
High St,
 Plymouth PL1 5 D5
High St,
 Stonehouse PL1 28 D3
Highbury Cres PL7 26 B2
Highclere Gdns PL6 12 C4
Higher Anderton Rd
 PL10 33 B2
Higher Brook Pk PL21 36 A2
Higher Churchway
 PL31 31 G4

Higher Compton Rd
 PL3 24 A2
Higher Efford Rd PL3 24 C4
Higher Kelly PL18 7 E7
Higher La PL1 5 D5
Higher Mowles PL3 24 C2
Higher Park Cl PL7 27 F5
Higher Port Vw PL12 15 E4
Higher Stert Ter PL4 30 A1
Higher Woodford La
 PL7 26 A1
Highfield Cl PL3 24 D3
Highfield Dr PL9 34 C1
Highfield Pk PL12 14 B3
Highglen Dr PL7 27 E2
Highland St PL21 36 C2
Hill Cl PL7 26 B4
Hill Crest PL3 23 H3
Hill La PL3 24 A2
Hill Park Cres PL4 4 E1
Hill Park Mews PL4 4 F2
Hill Path PL5 16 C1
Hill St PL4 4 E4
Hill Top Crest PL5 16 B4
Hillcrest Cl,
 Plympton PL7 27 E3
Hillcrest Cl,
 Wembury PL9 34 C2
Hillcrest Dr PL7 27 E4
Hilldale Rd PL31 31 E5
Hilldean Cl PL5 11 B5
Hillhead PL8 34 B6
Hillsborough PL4 24 A4
Hillsdunne Rd PL3 23 H2
Hillside Av,
 Plymouth PL4 23 G4
Hillside Av,
 Saltash PL12 15 F3
Hillside Cres PL31 31 F2
Hillside Dr PL8 35 B2
Hillside Rd PL31 15 E3
Hillside Way PL8 35 B3
Hilltop Cotts PL8 32 C3
Hilton Av PL5 17 F5
Hingston Ct PL6 18 B6
Hirmandale Rd PL5 16 D4
Hobart St PL1 29 E3
Hobbs Cres PL12 14 C3
Hodge Cl PL12 14 C4
Hoe App PL1 5 D6
Hoe Gdns PL1 5 D6
Hoe Rd PL1 5 B8
Hoe St PL1 5 D6
Hoegate Pl PL1 5 D6
Hoegate St PL1 5 D6
Hogarth Cl PL31 31 G5
Hogarth Walk PL31 31 G5
Holborn St PL4 29 H3
Holcombe Dr PL31 31 F6
Holcroft Cl PL12 14 D4
Holdsworth St PL4 4 B1
Holebay Cl PL31 31 F6
Holland Rd,
 Bodmin PL31 31 F4
Holland Rd,
 Langage PL7 27 G4
Holland Rd,
 Peverell PL3 23 H3
Holloway Gdns PL31 31 G6
Holly Ct PL6 25 F1
Holly Park Cl PL5 16 D1
Holly Park Dr PL5 16 D1
Hollycroft Rd PL3 24 B1
Holman Way PL21 36 A2
Holmans Bldgs PL1 28 A2
Holmbush Way PL8 32 D4
Holmer Down PL6 12 D5
Holmes Av PL4 24 C4
Holmwood Av PL31 31 E6
Holne Chase PL6 12 C5
Holtwood Dr PL21 36 A2
Holtwood Rd PL6 12 D6
Holwell Cl PL31 31 G6
Holyrood Pl PL1 5 B7
Home Farm Rd PL31 31 E3
Home Park Av PL3 23 H3
Home Park Rd PL12 15 F4
Home Pk PL2 22 D4
Home Sweet Home Ter
 PL4 30 A2
Homer Pk,
 Plymouth PL9 30 C5
Homer Pk,
 Saltash PL12 14 D3
Homer Pk La South
 PL9 30 C5
Homer Rise PL31 31 H4
Honcray PL9 30 D3
Honeysuckle Cl,
 Plymouth PL6 13 E5

Honeysuckle Cl,
 Saltash PL12 14 C2
Honicknowle Grn PL5 17 E4
Honicknowle La PL5 17 E5
Honiton Cl PL5 17 E3
Honiton Walk PL5 17 E2
Hooe Hill PL9 30 C6
Hooe Rd PL9 30 B5
Hooksbury Av PL7 27 F5
Hoopers La PL8 6 E2
Hopton Cl PL6 18 A6
Horn Cross Rd PL31 31 E3
Horn La,
 Bodmin PL31 31 E3
Horn La,
 Plymouth PL8 32 D4
Horn Lane Flats PL31 31 E4
Hornbeam Cl PL12 14 B3
Hornbrook Gdns PL6 11 C6
Hornby St PL2 22 C4
Hornchurch La PL5 16 B1
Hornchurch Rd PL5 16 B1
Horsham La,
 Honicknowle PL5 17 F4
Horsham La,
 Tamerton Foliot PL5 11 A5
Horswell Cl PL7 27 F3
Hosford Cl PL31 31 F6
Hospital Rd PL4 4 F2
Hotham Pl PL1 28 D1
Houldsworth Rd PL9 30 C3
Houndiscombe Rd
 PL4 4 D2
Hounster Dr PL10 33 A2
Hounster Hill PL10 33 A2
Housman Cl PL5 17 G4
How St PL4 5 E5
Howard Cl,
 Plymouth PL5 16 C4
Howard Cl,
 Saltash PL12 14 D4
Howard Ct PL1 5 A7
Howard Rd,
 Bodmin PL31 31 E2
Howard Rd,
 Plymouth PL9 30 D2
Howards Way PL21 36 A1
Humber Cl PL3 25 E2
Hungerford Rd PL21 23 E3
Hunsdon Rd PL21 35 D5
Hunter Cl PL6 18 A4
Hunters Cl PL21 36 B2
Huntingdon Gdns
 PL5 17 G2
Huntley Pl PL3 24 D4
Hurrabrook Cl PL6 19 F4
Hurrabrook Gdns
 PL6 19 F4
Hurrell Cl PL6 11 C6
Hurrell Ct PL3 24 C3
Hursley Bsns Pk
 PL6 13 E3
Hurst Cl PL31 31 F6
Hurst Rd PL31 31 E6
Hutchings Cl PL6 11 B6
Huxham Cl PL6 18 B6
Huxley Cl PL7 26 D2
Hyde Park Rd PL3 23 H3

Ilbert St PL1 4 A3
Ince Cl PL11 21 E5
Inchkeith Rd PL6 12 A6
Ingra Rd PL3 24 B2
Ingra Tor PL20 9 D5
Ingra Walk PL6 12 C4
Instow Walk PL5 16 D3
Insworke Cl PL10 33 C1
Insworke Cres PL10 33 C1
Insworke Pl PL10 33 C1
Inverdene PL3 23 G3
Ipswich Pl PL5 17 F2
Ivanhoe Rd PL5 16 A5
Ivybridge By-Pass
 PL21 36 B3
Ivydale Rd PL4 24 A4
Ivydene Rd PL21 36 B3

Jackmans Mdw PL10 33 C4
Jackson Cl PL5 16 C6
Jackson Pl PL2 22 C4
Jackson Way PL12 15 E3
Jago Av PL11 21 G6
James Cl PL31 31 H4
James Pl PL4 4 D2
James St,
 Devonport PL1 28 B3
James St,
 Plymouth PL4 4 D2
Jasmine Gdns,
 Chaddlewood PL7 27 F3

Jasmine Gdns,
 Glenholt PL6 13 F6
Jean Cres PL3 24 C2
Jedburgh Cres PL2 17 E6
Jeffery Cl PL6 11 C6
Jellicoe Rd PL5 17 H5
Jenkins Cl PL31 31 G5
Jennycliffe La PL9 30 A5
Jennyscombe Cl
 PL31 31 F6
Jephson Rd PL4 24 C6
Jessops PL7 26 B2
Jinkin Av PL4 24 A5
John St PL1 28 A1
Johnson Cl PL20 11 B2
Johnson Pk PL18 7 E7
Jordan La PL20 8 D2
Jubilee Cl,
 Ivybridge PL21 36 F2
Jubilee Cl,
 Saltash PL12 14 D4
Jubilee Cotts PL12 14 C5
Jubilee Rd PL5 16 C3
Jubilee Ter*,
 Sunnyside Rd PL4 24 C6
Julian Rd PL21 36 B2
Julian St PL4 30 A2
Julian Walk PL6 13 E6
Jump Cl PL6 12 D3
Juniper Way PL7 27 F3

Kathleaven St PL5 16 A5
Kay Cl PL7 26 D1
Keat St PL2 22 D1
Keaton Rd PL21 36 C3
Kedlestone Av PL5 16 D4
Kelly Cl PL5 21 H1
Kelvin Av PL4 24 B5
Kempe Cl PL2 22 C2
Kempton Ter PL11 21 G6
Kemyell Pl PL2 22 B5
Kendal Pl PL5 17 H2
Kenilworth Rd PL2 23 E1
Kenley Gdns PL5 16 C2
Kenmare Dr PL7 27 E4
Kenn Cl PL5 17 E3
Kennel Hill PL7 26 B4
Kennel Hill Cl PL7 26 B4
Kennel La PL7 26 A2
Kennet Cl PL3 24 C3
Kensington Pl PL4 24 A5
Kensington Rd PL4 4 F1
Kent Rd PL2 22 C4
Keppel Pl PL2 22 C4
Keppel St PL2 22 C5
Keppel Ct PL2 22 C4
Ker St PL1 28 B3
Ker Street Ope PL1 28 B3
Kerswick Cl PL12 14 D3
Kestrel Pk PL5 16 D6
Kestrel Way PL6 13 E4
Keswick Cres PL6 18 D4
Keyes Cl PL1 28 A3
Keyham Rd PL2 22 B4
Keyham St PL5 16 B6
Khyber Cl PL11 21 F5
Kidwelly Cl PL7 27 G4
Kiel Pl PL3 25 E4
Killigrew Av PL12 14 D5
Kiln Cl PL5 16 A6
Kimberley Villas PL21 36 B3
Kimberly Dr PL6 18 B5
King Edward Rd PL12 15 E4
King St,
 Gunnislake PL18 6 E1
King St,
 Millbrook PL10 33 B2
King St,
 Plymouth PL1 4 A4
King St, Torpoint PL11 21 H5
Kingfisher Cl PL6 13 E6
Kings Rd,
 Devonport PL1 28 C2
Kings Rd,
 Ernesettle PL5 16 C3
Kings Tamerton Rd
 PL5 16 C4
Kingsland Garden Cl
 PL3 23 H2
Kingsley Av PL31 31 H4
Kingsley Cl PL21 35 C5
Kingsley Rd PL4 23 H4
Kingsmill Rd PL12 14 C1
Kingston Cl PL7 27 E3
Kingston Dr PL7 27 E3
Kingsway Gdns PL5 17 H3
Kingswear Cres PL6 18 C6
Kingswood Park Av
 PL3 23 G2
Kingswood Rd PL18 6 E2

Kinnaird Cres PL6 11 D5
Kinross Av PL4 24 B5
Kinsale Rd PL5 16 C3
Kinterbury Rd PL5 15 H6
Kinterbury St PL1 5 D5
Kinterbury Ter PL5 15 H6
Kinver Cl PL6 19 E2
Kipling Gdns PL5 17 G4
Kirby Pl PL4 23 G6
Kirkby Pl PL4 4 D2
Kirkby Ter PL4 4 D2
Kirkdale Gdns PL2 23 E1
Kirkella Rd PL20 9 F6
Kirkland Cl PL6 12 D5
Kirkstall Cl PL2 22 D1
Kirkwall Rd PL5 17 H4
Kirton Pl PL3 24 C4
Kit Hill Cres PL5 15 H6
Kitley Way PL5 16 B6
Kitter Dr PL31 31 F5
Knapps Cl,
 Bodmin PL31 31 H4
Knapps Cl,
 Plymouth PL9 32 A2
Kneele Gdns PL3 17 H6
Knighton Hill PL9 34 D1
**Knighton Hill Bsns
 Centre** PL9 34 D1
Knighton Rd,
 Knighton PL9 34 C1
Knighton Rd,
 Plymouth PL4 24 A6
Knill Cross PL10 33 B2
Knowland Cl PL1 28 B2
Knowle Av PL2 22 C2
Kynance Cl PL11 21 E5

Laburnum Dr PL9 34 C2
Ladysmith Cl PL4 24 B5
Ladysmith Rd PL4 24 A5
Ladywell Av PL4 4 F3
Ladywell Pl PL4 4 F3
Laira Av PL3 24 D4
Laira Bridge Rd PL4 30 B1
Laira Gdns PL3 24 D4
Laira Park Cres PL4 24 C4
Laira Park Pl PL4 24 B4
Laira Park Rd PL4 24 B4
Laira Pl PL4 30 A1
Laira St PL4 30 A1
Laity Walk PL6 11 C6
Lake Rd PL9 30 B5
Lake View Dr PL5 16 D1
Lakeside Dr PL5 16 B1
Lalebrick Rd PL9 30 A5
Lambert Rd PL5 11 A6
Lambhay Hill PL1 5 E7
Lambhay St PL1 5 E7
Lamerton Cl PL5 17 E3
Lamorna Pk PL11 20 D5
Lancaster Gdns PL5 17 F2
Lander Rd PL12 15 F3
Langdon Down Way
 PL11 21 E5
Landrake Cl PL6 15 H6
Lands Pk PL31 31 E3
Landulph Gdns PL5 16 A6
Lang Gdns PL18 7 F7
Lang Gro PL31 31 H3
Langage Bsns Pk
 PL7 27 G4
Langage Ind Est
 PL7 27 H4
Langage Science Pk
 PL7 27 H3
Langdale Cl PL6 19 E5
Langdale Gdns PL6 18 D5
Langdon Cl PL31 31 H5
Langerwell Cl PL12 14 B4
Langerwell La PL12 14 B3
Langham Levels PL21 36 B3
Langham Pl PL4 30 A1
Langham Way PL21 36 B2
Langhill Rd PL3 23 G4
Langley Cl PL6 12 A5
Langley Cres PL6 12 A5
Langmead Cl PL6 18 C6
Langmead Rd PL6 18 C6
Langmore Cl PL6 24 B1
Langstone Rd PL2 23 F1
Langstone Ter PL2 23 F1
Langton Rd PL20 9 E6
Lanhydrock Rd PL4 24 B6
Lansdowne Rd PL6 18 A4
Larch Cl PL12 14 B3
Larch Dr PL6 13 F6
Lark Hill PL2 22 D2
Larkhall Rise PL3 24 C3
Larkham Cl PL7 26 A2
Larkham La PL7 26 A3

Mudge Way PL7 26 C3
Mudges Ter PL18 6 E1
Mulberry Cl PL6 13 E5
Mulberry Rd PL12 14 D5
Mulgrave St PL1 5 B6
Mullet Av PL3 24 D4
Mullet Cl PL3 24 D4
Mullet Rd PL3 24 D4
Mullion Cl PL11 21 E5
Murdock Rd PL11 21 E6
Mutley Plain, Mutley PL4 23 H4
Mutley Plain, Plymouth PL4 4 F1
Mutley Plain La PL4 23 H4
Mutley Rd PL3 23 H3
Mylor Cl PL2 17 G6
Myrtles Ct PL12 14 D2
Myrtleville PL2 22 D2

Nancarrows PL12 14 C5
Napier St PL1 28 C1
Napier Ter PL4 4 E1
Nash Cl PL7 27 E3
Navy Ter PL11 21 H6
Neal Cl PL7 27 F5
Neath Rd PL4 24 B6
Nelson Av PL1 28 C1
Nelson Gdns PL1 28 C1
Nelson St, Plymouth PL4 4 F3
Nelson St, Torpoint PL11 21 H6
Nelson Ter PL6 13 E6
Nepean St PL2 22 D3
Neptune Pk PL4 30 B3
Neswick St PL1 4 A4
Neswick Street Ope PL1 29 E2
Nettlehayes PL9 32 A2
Netton Cl PL31 31 H4
Nevada Cl PL3 25 E2
New Barn Hill PL7 26 C6
New Bri PL18 6 F1
New George St PL1 4 B4
New Mdw PL21 36 A1
New Park Rd PL7 27 E4
New Passage Hill PL1 28 A2
New Pk PL20 8 D3
New Rd, Plymouth PL6 12 D3
New Rd, Saltash PL12 14 C3
New Rd, Torpoint PL10 33 C5
New Rd, Yealmpton PL8 35 B2
New Rd, Yelverton PL20 11 A1
New Road Cl PL10 33 D5
New St, Plymouth PL1 5 E6
New St, Torpoint PL10 33 B2
New Wood Cl PL6 13 F4
Newbridge Hill PL18 6 E1
Newbury Cl PL5 17 E2
Newcastle Gdns PL5 17 E1
Newman Rd, Plymouth PL5 16 B4
Newman Rd, Saltash PL12 15 F3
Newnham Cl PL7 27 E1
Newnham Ind Est PL7 26 D2
Newnham Rd PL7 26 C2
Newnham Way PL7 26 D2
Newport St, Plymouth PL1 28 C3
Newport St, Torpoint PL10 33 B2
Newton Av PL5 16 C4
Newton Cl PL8 34 C5
Newton Gdns PL5 16 C5
Newton Hill PL8 34 C5
Nicholas Mdw PL17 7 A5
Nicholson Rd PL5 17 H4
Nightingale Cl PL9 32 A1
Nirvana Cl PL21 36 C2
Norfolk Cl PL3 24 D4
Norfolk Rd PL3 24 C4
Normandy Hill PL5 15 G4
Normandy Way PL5 15 H5
North Cross PL1 4 C3
North Devon Pl PL4 4 E1
North Down Cres PL2 22 C3
North Down Gdns PL2 22 C3
North Down Rd PL2 23 E2
North Hill PL4 4 E3
North Park Villas PL12 14 C2
North Prospect Rd PL2 16 C6
North Quay PL4 5 E5
North Rd, Ivybridge PL21 35 B4
North Rd, Saltash PL12 15 F3
North Rd, Torpoint PL11 21 G6
North Rd, Yelverton PL20 8 D4
North Rd East PL4 4 C2
North Rd West PL1 4 A3
North St PL4 5 F5
North Weald Gdns PL5 16 B1
Northampton Cl PL5 17 E1
Northesk St PL2 22 D4
Northolt Av PL5 16 A2
Northumberland St PL5 16 B6
Northumberland Ter PL1 5 A8
Norton Av PL4 24 B5
Norwich Av PL5 16 D1
Notre Dame Cl PL6 18 A2
Notte St PL1 5 B6
Novorossisk Rd PL6 18 D5
Nursery Cl PL5 11 A6

Oak Apple Cl PL12 14 D2
Oak Dr PL6 17 H3
Oak Gdns PL21 36 E3
Oak Tree Pk PL6 19 E1
Oakapple Cl PL7 25 H2
Oakcroft Rd PL2 23 E2
Oakdene Rise PL31 31 F4
Oakey Orchard PL17 7 A6
Oakfield Cl PL7 27 G2
Oakfield Pl PL4 30 B2
Oakfield Rd PL7 26 A3
Oakfield Terrace Rd PL4 30 A1
Oakham Rd PL5 17 E1
Oaklands Cl PL6 12 D5
Oaklands Dr PL12 14 C4
Oaklands Grn PL12 14 C4
Oaktree Cl PL21 36 A2
Oaktree Ct PL6 18 A5
Oakwood Cl PL6 13 E5
Oates Rd PL2 23 E3
Ocean St PL2 22 B2
Octagon St PL1 29 E2
Okehampton Cl PL7 27 F4
Okehampton Way PL21 36 D3
Old Chapel Way PL10 33 B1
Old Farm Rd PL5 16 A6
Old Ferry Rd PL12 15 F3
Old George St PL1 5 B5
Old Laira Rd PL3 24 B4
Old Mill Ct PL7 26 C3
Old Mine La PL18 6 A3
Old Park Rd PL3 23 G3
Old Priory PL7 26 B3
Old Rd PL8 32 E4
Old School Rd PL5 16 A6
Old Station Rd PL20 8 C3
Old Town St PL1 5 D5
Old Warleigh La PL5 10 D5
Old Woodlands Rd PL5 17 F3
Oldlands Cl PL6 12 C6
Onslow Rd PL2 23 F2
Orchard Av PL6 24 C1
Orchard Cl, Langage PL7 27 G3
Orchard Cl, Yealmpton PL8 35 B2
Orchard Cres PL9 30 C3
Orchard Ct PL21 36 B3
Orchard La PL7 26 C2
Orchard Rd PL2 23 E2
Orchardton Ter PL31 31 F5
Orchid Av PL21 36 A2
Ordnance St PL1 28 A2
Oregon Way PL3 24 D2
Oreston Rd PL9 30 C3
Osborne Pl PL1 5 C7
Osborne Rd PL3 22 D5
Oscar Way PL7 27 G3
Osprey Gdns PL9 32 A1
Outland Rd PL2 23 E3
Overdale Rd PL2 22 D1
Overton Gdns PL3 24 A3
Oxford Av PL3 23 H3
Oxford Gdns PL3 23 H3
Oxford Pl PL1 4 B3
Oxford St PL1 4 B3
Oxford Ter PL1 4 B3
Packington St PL2 22 D4
Paddock Cl, Bodmin PL31 31 E6
Paddock Cl, Saltash PL12 14 C2
Paddock Dr PL21 36 D3
Palace St PL1 5 D5
Palmer Cl PL7 27 F4
Palmerston St PL1 28 D1
Paper Makers La PL21 36 E2
Parade Rd PL5 16 D3
Paradise Pl PL1 28 C1
Paradise Rd PL1 28 B2
Park Av, Devonport PL1 28 B1
Park Av, Plymstock PL9 30 D4
Park Cl, Ivybridge PL21 36 C2
Park Cl, Plymouth PL7 25 H2
Park Cres PL9 30 C3
Park Hill Ter PL18 7 E7
Park La PL9 30 C3
Park Pl PL3 22 D4
Park Place La PL3 22 D5
Park Rd, Plymouth PL3 24 A3
Park Rd, Torpoint PL11 21 G6
Park St, Ivybridge PL21 36 C3
Park St, Plymouth PL3 22 D4
Park Street Ope PL3 22 D4
Park Ter PL4 4 F4
Park Vw PL4 24 B6
Parker Cl PL7 25 H4
Parker Rd PL2 23 E2
Parkers Grn PL18 6 D2
Parkesway PL12 14 D5
Parkfield Dr PL6 19 F5
Parkside, Ivybridge PL21 36 E3
Parkside, Plymouth PL2 22 C3
Parkstone La PL7 26 D3
Parkway, Manadon PL6 18 A6
Parkway, St Budeaux PL5 16 A4
Parkway Ct PL6 25 E1
Parkway Ind Est PL6 25 F1
Parkwood Cl PL6 12 B2
Parnell Cl PL6 18 A6
Parr La PL4 29 H3
Parr St PL4 29 H3
Parsonage Rd PL8 34 C5
Parsons Cl PL31 31 F6
Pasley St PL2 22 C4
Pasley St East PL2 22 C4
Passage Wood Rd PL8 34 A6
Patna Pl PL1 4 A3
Patterdale Cl PL6 19 E3
Patterdale Walk PL6 19 E3
Pattinson Cl PL6 19 F4
Pattinson Dr PL6 19 F4
Paynter Walk PL7 27 F4
Peacock Av PL11 21 G6
Peacock Cl PL7 26 D2
Peacock La PL4 5 D5
Pearn Gdns PL3 24 A2
Pearn Rd PL3 24 A1
Pearn Ridge PL3 24 A2
Pearson Av PL4 24 A4
Pearson Rd PL4 24 A4
Peeks Av PL31 31 F4
Peel St PL1 28 D3
Peel Street Flats PL1 28 D3
Pellew Pl PL2 22 C4
Pembrey Walk PL5 16 B3
Pembroke La PL1 28 B3
Pembroke St PL1 28 B3
Pemros Rd PL5 15 H5
Pencair Av PL11 21 E6
Pencreber Rd PL20 8 C3
Pendeen Cl PL6 12 A6
Pendeen Cres PL6 12 A6
Pendennis Cl, Plymouth PL3 24 A1
Pendennis Cl, Torpoint PL11 21 E5
Pendilly Av PL11 21 E6
Pengelly Cl PL11 21 F3
Pengelly Hill PL11 21 F3
Pengelly Pk PL11 21 F3
Penlee Gdns PL3 22 D5
Penlee Pk PL11 21 E5
Penlee Pl PL4 24 A4
Penlee Rd PL3 22 D5
Penlee Way PL3 22 D5
Pennant Way PL21 35 C5
Pennycomequick Hill PL3 4 B2
Pennycross Cl PL2 23 G1
Pennycross Park Rd PL2 23 F1
Pennys La PL9 32 A2
Penrith Cl PL6 18 D3
Penrith Gdns PL6 18 D3
Penrith Walk PL6 18 D3
Penrose St PL1 4 A3
Penrose Villas PL4 24 A4
Pentamar St PL2 22 C5
Pentillie Cres PL3 23 G4
Pentillie Rd, Plymouth PL4 23 H5
Pentillie Rd, Yelverton PL20 11 B3
Pentire Rd PL11 21 F5
Pentland Cl PL6 12 A5
Pentyre Ter PL4 24 A5
Pepper La PL9 32 B1
Pepys Pl PL5 17 G6
Percy St PL5 16 A5
Percy Ter PL4 24 B4
Periwinkle Dr PL7 27 G3
Perranporth Cl PL5 16 B3
Perryman Cl PL7 26 C1
Peters Cl PL31 31 H3
Peters Park Cl PL5 16 B5
Peters Park La PL5 16 A4
Petersfield Cl PL3 24 C2
Pethick Cl PL6 11 C6
Pethill Cl PL6 19 G4
Peverell Park Rd PL3 23 G1
Peverell Ter PL3 23 G3
Pew Tor Cl PL20 9 D5
Philip Cl PL31 31 F4
Philip Gdns PL31 31 F4
Phillimore St PL2 22 C4
Phoenix Cl PL20 8 C3
Phoenix St PL1 29 E3
Pick Pie Dr PL6 13 E5
Pier La PL10 33 D6
Pier St PL1 5 A7
Pike Rd PL3 24 D4
Pilgrim Cl PL2 23 E3
Pilgrim Dr PL20 11 C2
Pill La PL12 15 E2
Pillar Walk PL6 11 D5
Pillmere Dr PL12 14 C2
Pillory Hill PL8 34 C6
Pin La PL1 5 E6
Pine Vw PL18 6 F2
Pinehurst Way PL21 36 A2
Pinewood Cl PL7 26 D2
Pinewood Dr PL6 13 F5
Pipit Dr PL6 13 E4
Place De Brest PL1 4 C4
Plaistow Cl PL5 16 C4
Plaistow Cres PL5 16 B4
Pleasure Hill Cl PL9 30 D2
Plintona Vw PL7 26 C1
Plougastel Dr PL12 15 E4
Plough Grn PL12 14 C3
Ploughboy Mews PL12 14 B3
Ploughman Way PL8 35 C2
Plover Rise PL21 36 B2
Plumer Rd PL6 17 H4
Plym St PL4 4 F3
Plymbridge Gdns PL7 26 A2
Plymbridge La PL6 18 B2
Plymbridge Rd, Plymouth PL6 12 C6
Plymbridge Rd, Plympton PL7 26 A1
Plymouth Bsns Pk PL6 18 A3
Plymouth La PL20 9 E6
Plymouth Rd, Crabtree PL3,7 25 E4
Plymouth Rd, Plympton PL7 26 A3
Plymouth Rd, Yelverton PL20 9 D7
Plympton By-Pass PL7 25 G3
Plympton Hill PL7 26 D6
Plymstock Rd, Bodmin PL31 31 E3
Plymstock Rd, Plymouth PL9 30 C3
Plymtree Dr PL7 26 A1
Pocklington Rise PL7 26 C4
Pode Dr PL7 27 F4
Pollard Cl, Plymouth PL9 30 B5
Pollard Cl, Saltash PL12 14 B4
Pollards Ct PL12 14 D2
Pollards Way PL12 14 D3
Polruan Ter PL1 28 D2
Polsporder Pl PL10 33 C5
Polzeath Gdns PL2 17 G6
Pomphlett Cl PL9 30 D3
Pomphlett Farm Ind Est PL31 31 E2
Pomphlett Gdns PL9 30 D2
Pomphlett Rd, Bodmin PL31 31 E3
Pomphlett Rd, Plymouth PL9 30 D2
Pondfield Rd PL12 14 B3
Ponsonby Rd PL3 23 E4
Poole Park Rd PL5 15 H6
Poplar Cl PL7 27 F3
Porsham Cl PL6 12 C3
Porsham La PL5 11 C5
Portal Pl PL21 36 B3
Porteous Cl PL1 28 B2
Portland Ct PL1 28 B1
Portland Pl PL4 23 G6
Portland Pl East PL4 4 D2
Portland Rd PL1 28 B1
Portland Sq PL4 4 D3
Portland Villas PL4 4 C2
Portway Cl PL9 32 A2
Potters Way PL7 26 B3
Pottery Rd PL1 28 A1
Poultney Cl PL7 27 E3
Pound Farm La PL21 36 C2
Pound Rd PL20 9 A5
Pound St PL1 28 D4
Pounds Park Rd, Plymouth PL3 23 G2
Pounds Park Rd, Yelverton PL20 11 B1
Pounds Pk PL12 15 F3
Powderham Rd PL3 23 H1
Powis Gdns PL5 17 E4
Powisland Dr PL6 18 A1
Prestonbury Cl PL6 12 C5
Prideaux Cl PL12 14 C1
Prideaux Rd PL21 36 E2
Pridham La PL2 23 F1
Priesthood Ter PL10 33 A2
Priestley Av PL5 16 C4
Primrose Cl, Ivybridge PL21 36 D3
Primrose Cl, Torpoint PL11 21 E5
Primrose Mdw PL21 36 A2
Primrose Walk PL12 14 C2
Prince Maurice Rd PL4 24 A5
Princes Rd PL6 19 E1
Princes St PL1 28 B2
Princess Av, Bodmin PL31 31 E4
Princess Av, Plymouth PL5 16 D3
Princess Cres PL31 31 E4
Princess St PL1 5 C5
Princess Way PL1 5 B5
Princetown Rd PL20 9 F5
Priors Pk PL31 31 G2
Priory Cl PL21 36 B2
Priory Dr PL7 26 C4
Priory Lawn Ter PL3 24 B3
Priory Mill PL7 26 B3
Priory Rd PL3 24 B3
Priory Ridge PL7 26 B3
Prospect La PL12 14 B3
Prospect Pl PL1 5 A6
Prospect Row PL1 28 B3
Prospect St PL4 4 F3
Prospect Walk PL12 14 B4
Prouse Cres PL2 17 F6
Prouse Rise PL12 15 E4
Providence Pl, Calstock PL18 7 F7
Providence Pl, Plymouth PL1 28 C1
Providence St PL4 4 E2
Prynne Cl PL1 4 A4
Pump Hill PL9 34 A2
Pykes Down PL21 36 F3
Pym St PL1 28 B1
Pyne Villas PL9 30 B4

Quarry Cotts PL5 17 E4
Quarry La PL18 6 D2
Quarry Park Av PL9 30 D4
Quarry Park Rd, Peverell PL3 23 G3

Quarry Park Rd, Plymstock PL9 30 D4
Quarry St PL11 21 H5
Quay Rd PL1 5 E6
Queen Anne Ter PL4 4 E3
Queen Annes Pl PL4 29 H4
Queen St PL1 28 A2
Queens Cl PL6 19 E1
Queens Gate, Lipson PL4 24 A5
Queens Gate, Stoke PL1 29 E1
Queens Gate Mews PL4 24 A5
Queens Gate Villas PL4 24 A5
Queens Rd, Ernesettle PL5 16 C3
Queens Rd, Lipson PL4 24 A5

Radcliffe Cl PL6 11 D6
Radford Av PL4 30 B1
Radford La PL10 33 A3
Radford Park Dr PL9 30 D4
Radford Park Rd, Bodmin PL31 31 E4
Radford Park Rd, Plymouth PL9 30 D5
Radford Rd PL1 5 A7
Radford Vw PL9 30 D5
Radnor Pl PL4 4 E4
Radnor St PL4 4 E3
Raglan Ct PL1 28 C3
Raglan Gdns PL1 28 B3
Raglan Rd PL1 28 B2
Railway Cotts PL2 22 C3
Raleigh Ct PL7 27 F3
Raleigh Rd PL21 36 A1
Raleigh St PL1 5 B5
Ramage Cl PL6 19 G3
Ramillies Av PL5 16 D3
Ramsey Gdns PL5 17 G5
Randwick Park Rd PL9 30 D3
Raphael Cl PL31 31 G5
Raphael Dr PL31 31 G5
Rashleigh Av, Plymouth PL7 26 C1
Rashleigh Av, Saltash PL12 14 D5
Rawlin Cl PL6 18 D6
Raymond Way PL7 26 B2
Raynham Rd PL3 23 E5
Reading Walk PL5 17 F2
Recreation Rd PL2 23 F1
Rectory Rd PL1 28 C2
Red Lion Hill PL8 32 E3
Reddicliff Cl PL9 30 D6
Reddicliff Rd PL9 30 C5
Reddington Rd PL3 24 B1
Redhill Cl PL5 16 B2
Redruth Cl PL5 16 D1
Redvers Gro PL7 26 C4
Redwing Dr PL6 13 E4
Redwood Dr PL7 27 F3
Regent Ct PL4 4 E4
Regent St PL4 4 D4
Reigate Rd PL31 31 E3
Rendle St PL1 5 A5
Rendlesham Gdns PL6 19 E3
Rennie Av PL5 15 H5
Renoir Cl PL31 31 G5
Renown St PL2 22 B2
Research Way PL6 18 C2
Reservoir Cres PL31 31 H3
Reservoir Rd, Bodmin PL31 31 G4
Reservoir Rd, Plymouth PL3 24 A2
Reservoir Way PL31 31 H3
Restormel Rd PL4 4 D1
Restormel Ter PL4 4 D1
Resvervoir La PL3 24 A2
Revel Rd PL3 24 B2
Revell Park Rd PL7 26 B2
Revelstoke Rd PL8 34 C6
Reynolds Gro PL5 15 H6
Reynolds Rd PL7 26 A2
Rheola Gdns PL6 19 E3
Rhodes Cl PL7 26 C1
Ribble Gdns PL3 24 D2
Richards Row PL3 23 H1
Richards Ter PL10 33 A2
Richmond Rd PL6 18 A4
Richmond Walk PL1 28 B4
Ridge Park Av PL4 4 C1
Ridge Park Rd PL7 26 C3
Ridge Pk PL7 26 C3
Ridge Rd PL7 26 A5
Ridgeway, Plymouth PL7 26 B3
Ridgeway, Saltash PL12 14 D5
Riga Ter PL3 24 C4
Rigdale Cl PL6 24 B1
Ringmore Way PL5 16 D2
Risdon Av PL4 30 B1
River Plym PL4 24 D6
River Vw, Plymouth PL4 30 B1
River Vw, Saltash PL12 15 F3
Riverford Cl PL6 12 D5
Rivers Cl PL21 36 E2
Riverside Bsns Pk PL1 28 A1
Riverside Cotts PL12 15 F3
Riverside Pl PL1 28 A2
Riverside Rd East PL8 34 C5
Riverside Rd West PL8 34 B6
Riverside Walk, Tamerton Foliot PL5 11 A6
Riverside Walk, Yealmpton PL8 35 C2
Robert Adams Cl PL7 25 H4
Roberts Av PL11 21 G6
Roberts Rd PL5 16 A6
Roborough Av PL6 18 B1
Roborough Cl PL6 18 C1
Roborough La PL5 11 B5
Robyns Cl PL7 27 F4
Rochester Rd PL4 4 E1
Rochford Cres PL5 16 C1
Rock Gdns PL9 30 D2
Rock Ter PL7 26 B4
Rockdale Rd PL8 35 C2
Rockfield Av PL6 11 D6
Rockhill PL5 11 B5
Rockingham Rd PL3 24 B4
Rockville Pk PL31 31 E3
Rockwood Rd PL6 13 F4
Rocky Park Av PL9 30 D3
Rocky Park Rd PL31 31 E3
Rodda Cl PL18 6 E1
Roddick Way PL7 27 G3
Rodgers Dr PL12 14 D3
Rodney St PL5 22 B1
Roeselare Av PL11 21 G5
Roeselare Cl PL11 21 G6
Rogate Dr PL6 18 D2
Rogate Walk PL6 18 D2
Rollis Park Cl PL9 30 C3
Rollis Park Rd PL9 30 C3
Rolston Cl PL6 11 C6
Roman Rd PL5 16 B5
Roman Way PL5 16 B4
Romilly Gdns PL7 25 H4
Romney Cl PL5 17 E5
Ronald Ter PL2 22 C4
Ronsdale Cl PL9 30 D3
Roope Cl PL5 22 A1
Rope Walk PL4 5 F7
Roper Av PL9 30 D3
Rorkes Cl PL5 16 B4
Rose Cotts PL6 18 C6
Rose Gdns PL6 19 E1
Rose Hill PL9 34 C2
Rose Hill Cotts PL1 28 D1
Rosebery Av PL4 24 B5
Rosebery La PL4 24 B5
Rosebery Rd PL4 24 A6
Roseclave Cl PL7 27 G3
Rosedale Av PL2 23 F1
Rosedown Av PL2 22 D2
Rosehip Cl PL6 13 E5
Rosevean Gdns PL3 24 A3
Roseveare Cl PL31 31 G3
Rosewood Cl PL31 31 F5
Rospeath Cres PL2 17 G6
Ross St PL2 22 C5
Rosslyn Park Rd PL3 23 G3
Rothbury Cl PL6 19 E2
Rothbury Gdns PL6 19 E2
Rothesay Gdns PL5 17 F3
Rougemont Cl PL3 24 C2
Roundsnest PL8 35 B2
Row Down Cl PL7 27 H4
Row La PL5 16 B4
Rowan Cl PL7 27 F3
Rowan Ct PL12 14 B4
Rowan Way PL6 13 E5
Rowden St PL3 23 H3
Rowe St, Plymouth PL4 4 D3
Rowe St, Torpoint PL11 21 H5
Rowland Cl PL31 31 E6
Rowse Gdns PL18 7 F7
Royal Navy Av PL2 22 B3
Royal Par PL1 5 B5
Royal William Rd PL1 28 D4
Rudyerd Walk PL3 24 D3
Rue St Pierre PL21 36 E2
Rufford Cl PL2 22 D1
Rush Park Ter PL18 6 E1
Ruskin Cres PL5 17 G4
Russell Av PL3 23 H1
Russell Cl, Bodmin PL31 31 G3
Russell Cl, Gunnislake PL18 6 E1
Russell Cl, Saltash PL12 14 C4
Russell Pl PL4 4 B1
Russet Wood PL5 16 C2
Rutger Pl PL1 28 D1
Ruthven Cl PL6 18 A6
Rutland Rd PL4 24 A4
Rydal Cl PL6 18 D4
Ryder Rd PL2 22 C4
Rye Hill PL12 14 B4
Ryeland Cl PL9 34 C2

St Albans Pk PL20 9 F7
St Andrew Pl PL10 33 C6
St Andrew St PL1 5 D6
St Andrews Cl, Calstock PL18 7 F7
St Andrews Cl, Saltash PL12 14 C4
St Andrews Cl, Yelverton PL20 11 C2
St Andrews Cross PL1 5 D5
St Andrews Pl PL1 5 D5
St Andrews St, Cawsand PL10 33 C6
St Andrews St, Millbrook PL10 33 A2
St Annes Rd, Plymouth PL6 18 D1
St Annes Rd, Saltash PL12 14 D3
St Aubyn Av PL2 22 C3
St Aubyn Rd PL1 28 A2
St Aubyn St PL1 28 B2
St Austin Cl PL21 36 B2
St Barnabas Ter PL1 29 E1
St Boniface Cl PL2 23 F1
St Boniface Dr PL2 23 F1
St Bridget Av PL6 17 H6
St Budeaux By-Pass PL5 16 C6
St Catherines Pk PL8 34 C4
St Dunstans Ter PL4 24 B6
St Edward Gdns PL6 18 B6
St Elizabeth Cl PL7 26 D5
St Erth Rd PL2 23 G1
St Eval Pl PL5 16 C2
St Francis Ct PL5 17 E4
St Gabriels Av PL3 23 G4
St Georges Av PL2 23 F1
St Georges Rd PL12 14 D3
St Georges Ter PL2 22 C4
St Helens Walk PL5 17 F2
St Hilary Ter PL4 24 A6
St James Pl East PL1 5 B6
St James Pl West PL1 5 B6
St James Rd PL11 21 H6
St Johns Bridge Rd PL4 29 H3
St Johns Cl, Ivybridge PL21 36 B3
St Johns Cl, Plymouth PL6 18 D2
St Johns Cl, Torpoint PL10 33 B2
St Johns Dr PL9 30 B5
St Johns Rd, Cattedown PL4 29 H3
St Johns Rd, Ivybridge PL21 36 B2
St Johns Rd, Torpoint PL10 33 B1
St Johns Rd, Turnchapel PL9 30 A4
St Johns Rd, Yelverton PL20 8 D3
St Johns St PL4 29 H3
St Josephs Cl PL6 18 A6
St Judes Rd PL4 29 H3
St Keverne Pl PL2 17 G6
St Lawrence Rd PL4 4 D1
St Leo Pl PL2 22 B4
St Leonards Rd PL4 30 A1
St Levan Rd PL2 22 B4
St Margarets Rd PL7 25 H2
St Marks Rd PL6 18 D1
St Martins Av PL3 23 G1
St Mary St PL1 28 D3
St Marys Cl PL7 26 B3
St Marys Ct PL7 26 B3
St Marys Rd PL7 26 A2
St Maurice Mews PL7 26 C4
St Maurice Rd PL7 26 D5
St Maurice Vw PL7 27 F5
St Mawes Ter*, Cotehele Av PL2 22 C3
St Michael Av PL2 22 C3
St Michaels Cl PL1 28 B3
St Michaels Ter PL1 28 C1
St Modwen Rd PL6 25 F1
St Nazaire App PL1 28 B2
St Pancras Av PL2 17 F6
St Pauls Cl PL3 24 C3
St Pauls St PL1 28 D4
St Peters Cl, Plymouth PL1 29 E2
St Peters Cl, Plympton PL7 26 D5
St Peters Rd PL5 17 F4
St Peters Way PL21 36 E3
St Simons La PL4 24 B5
St Stephens Hill PL12 14 C5
St Stephens Pl PL7 26 C3
St Stephens Rd, Plymouth PL7 26 D5
St Stephens Rd, Saltash PL12 14 D5
St Stephens St PL1 28 B3
St Thomas Cl PL7 26 D5
St Vincent St PL2 22 C4
St Werburgh Cl PL9 34 C3
Salamanca St PL11 21 H6
Salcombe Rd PL4 24 A5
Salcombe Ter PL4 24 A5
Salisbury Ope PL3 23 E4
Salisbury Rd PL4 24 A6
Saltash Bsns Pk PL12 14 B2
Saltash By-Pass PL12 14 A2
Saltash Ind Est PL12 14 C2
Saltash Parkway Ind Est PL12 14 B2
Saltash Pass PL5 15 H4
Saltash Rd, Keyham PL2 22 B3
Saltash Rd, Plymouth PL3 4 B2
Saltburn Rd PL5 16 A5
Saltmill La PL12 15 E2
Saltram Ter PL7 26 C3
Sampford Gdns PL20 8 E2
Sampson Cl PL18 6 A3
San Sabastian Sq PL1 5 C6
Sand Hill PL18 6 E3
Sand La PL18 7 E7
Sandford Rd PL31 31 F3
Sandon Walk PL6 18 B6
Sandquay La PL12 15 F4
Sandy La PL21 36 D2
Sandy Rd PL7 27 G5
Sango Ct PL10 33 C1
Sango Rd PL11 21 G6
Sarah Cl PL20 11 B2
Sarum Cl PL3 24 A1
Saunders Walk PL6 11 C6
Savage Rd PL5 22 A1
Savery Cl PL21 36 E2
Savery Ter PL4 24 B5
Sawrey St PL1 29 E3
School Cl PL7 26 B2
School Dr PL6 13 E5
School La PL7 26 C4
Sconner Rd PL11 21 G5
Scott Av PL5 15 H6
Scott Rd PL2 23 E3
Sea View Av PL4 24 A5
Sea View Dr PL9 34 C2
Sea View Ter PL4 24 A6
Seacroft Rd PL5 16 A4
Seaton Av PL4 23 H4
Seaton Bsns Pk PL6 18 B3
Seaton La PL4 23 H4
Seaton Pl PL2 22 C3
Seaton Way PL20 9 A6
Second Av, Bodmin PL31 31 F2
Second Av, Camels Head PL2 22 C1
Second Av, Plymouth PL1 28 C2
Sedge Cl PL21 36 E3
Sedley Way PL5 17 G4
Sefton Av PL4 24 B5
Sefton Cl PL4 24 B5
Segrave Rd PL2 23 E3
Selkirk Pl PL5 17 H4
Sellon Ct PL1 4 A4
Selsden Cl PL31 31 H4
Sennen Cl PL11 21 F5
Sennen Pl PL2 22 B4
Serpell Cl PL6 11 D6
Seven Stars La PL5 11 A6
Seven Trees Ct PL4 4 F2
Severn Pl PL3 24 C3
Seymour Av PL4 24 A6
Seymour Dr PL3 24 A3
Seymour Mews PL4 24 A6
Seymour Pk PL3 24 A4
Seymour Rd, Mannamead PL3 24 A3
Seymour Rd, Plympton PL7 26 A2
Seymour St PL4 4 F3
Shaftesbury Cotts PL4 4 F2
Shakespeare Rd PL5 17 E4
Shaldon Cres PL5 17 E3
Shallowford Cl PL6 24 D1
Shallowford Rd PL6 24 D1
Shapleys Gdns PL31 31 G5
Shapters Rd PL4 30 A2
Shapters Way PL4 30 B2
Sharon Way PL6 18 B1
Sharrose Rd PL9 30 B5
Shaw Way PL9 30 A4
Shearwood Cl PL7 26 A2
Sheepstor Rd PL6 19 E5
Shell Cl PL6 19 F5
Shelley Way PL5 16 B5
Shepherds La PL4 29 H3
Sherborne Cl PL9 32 A2
Sherford Cres, Elburton PL9 32 A2
Sherford Cres, Ernesettle PL5 16 D4
Sherford Rd PL9 32 A2
Sherford Walk PL9 32 B2
Sheridan Rd PL5 17 F5
Sherrell Pk PL20 11 B2
Sherril Cl PL31 31 F6
Sherwell Hill PL21 36 F4
Sherwell La PL4 4 D2
Sherwill Cl PL21 36 A2
Shipley Walk PL6 18 B6
Shirburn Rd PL6 18 C6
Shirley Gdns PL5 17 F5
Short Cotts PL11 21 G6
Short Park Rd PL3 23 G3
Shortwood Cres PL31 31 F3
Shrewsbury Rd PL5 17 E2
Shute Park Rd PL31 31 F5
Silver Birch Cl PL6 12 D5
Silver St, Saltash PL12 15 G4
Silver St, Yelverton PL20 10 C1
Silver Ter PL10 33 D1
Simon Cl PL31 31 E4
Sims Ter PL18 6 F2
Sir Hawkins Sq PL1 5 D5
Sithney St PL5 16 A6
Six O' Clock La PL7 26 C5
Skardale Gdns PL6 25 E1
Skardon Pl PL4 4 E2
Skerries Rd PL6 12 A5
Skinnard La PL18 6 D4
Skylark Rise PL6 13 E4
Slade Cl PL31 31 F5
Slatelands Cl PL7 27 F5
Sleep Cl PL12 14 B3
Slipperstone Dr PL21 36 A2
Smallack Cl PL6 18 A4
Smallack Dr PL6 18 A4
Smallridge Cl PL31 31 F6
Smeaton Sq PL3 24 D3
Smithfield Dr PL12 14 B3
Smiths Way PL12 14 B3
Smithy Cl PL12 14 C3
Snell Dr PL12 14 B3
Somerset Cotts PL3 22 D4
Somerset Pl PL3 22 D5
South Down Rd PL2 23 E2
South Hill, Devonport PL1 28 C1
South Hill, Hooe PL9 30 C5
South Milton St PL4 30 A2
South View Cl PL7 26 C1
South View Pk PL7 26 B1
South View Ter PL4 24 B6
South Vw, Bodmin PL31 31 H4
South Vw, Plymouth PL5 17 H4
South Vw, Torpoint PL10 33 C1

South Vw,
  Yelverton PL20 — 8 C2
Southdown Rd PL10 — 33 B1
Southdown Ter PL10 — 33 C1
Southella Rd PL20 — 9 F6
Southern Cl PL2 — 22 C1
Southern Ter PL4 — 24 A5
Southernway PL31 — 31 F3
Southfield PL12 — 14 C4
Southgate Av PL31 — 31 E6
Southgate Cl PL31 — 31 E6
Southland Park Cres
  PL9 — 34 B2
Southland Park Rd
  PL9 — 34 B3
Southside St PL1 — 5 D6
Southway Dr PL6 — 17 G1
Southway La,
  Tamerton Foliot PL6 — 11 B6
Southway La,
  Widewell PL6 — 12 B5
Southwell Rd PL6 — 17 H6
Sovereign Ct PL7 — 26 A4
Sparke Cl PL7 — 27 F4
Speakers Rd PL21 — 36 E2
Speedwell Cl PL10 — 33 C2
Speedwell Cres PL21 — 24 B1
Speedwell Walk PL6 — 24 B1
Spencer Gdns PL12 — 15 E5
Spencer Rd PL31 — 31 E2
Spire Hill Pk PL12 — 14 C4
Spring Pk PL6 — 13 E5
Springfield Av PL31 — 31 G4
Springfield Cl PL31 — 31 G4
Springfield Dr PL3 — 22 D4
Springfield La PL31 — 31 G3
Springfield Rd PL31 — 31 G4
Springfield Rise PL31 — 31 G4
Springhill PL2 — 17 F6
Springhill Grn PL2 — 17 F6
Springwood Cl,
  Ivybridge PL21 — 36 E2
Springwood Cl,
  Plymouth PL7 — 27 E5
Spruce Gdns PL7 — 27 F3
Staddiscombe Rd
  PL31 — 31 F6
Staddon Cres PL31 — 31 E5
Staddon Grn PL9 — 30 D5
Staddon Park Rd
  PL31 — 31 E5
Staddon Terrace La
  PL1 — 4 B2
Stag La PL31 — 31 F3
Stamford Cl PL9 — 30 A5
Stamford La PL9 — 30 A5
Stamford Rd PL9 — 30 A4
Stamps Hill PL8 — 32 E2
Stanborough Rd PL31 — 31 F3
Stanbury Av PL6 — 17 H5
Standarhay Cl PL9 — 32 A1
Standarhay Villas
  PL31 — 31 H3
Stangray Av PL4 — 23 H1
Stanhope Rd PL5 — 15 H5
Staniforth Dr PL21 — 36 D3
Stanlake Cl PL12 — 14 D4
Stanley Pl PL4 — 24 C6
Stannary Cl PL21 — 36 F2
Staple Cl PL12 — 12 C4
Stapleford Gdns PL5 — 16 C2
Station La PL18 — 7 F7
Station Rd,
  Bere Alston PL20 — 11 A1
Station Rd,
  Bere Ferrers PL20 — 10 C1
Station Rd,
  Elburton PL9 — 32 A1
Station Rd,
  Gunnislake PL18 — 6 D3
Station Rd,
  Horrabridge PL20 — 8 C3
Station Rd,
  Ivybridge PL21 — 36 D2
Station Rd,
  Keyham PL2 — 22 B3
Station Rd,
  Plympton PL7 — 26 C3
Station Rd,
  Saltash PL12 — 15 F4
Station Rd,
  Tamerton Foliot PL5 — 10 B6
Station Rd,
  Yelverton PL20 — 9 E6
Steeple Cl PL31 — 31 F6
Steer Park Rd PL7 — 27 G3
Steer Point Rd PL8 — 32 D4
Stefan Cl PL9 — 30 B5
Stenlake Pl PL4 — 24 C6
Stenlake Ter PL4 — 30 B1

Stentaway Cl PL31 — 31 F3
Stentaway Dr PL31 — 31 F3
Stentaway Rd PL31 — 31 F3
Stephenson Way PL5 — 16 C4
Stibb La PL21 — 35 D4
Stillman Ct PL4 — 5 E5
Stillman St PL4 — 5 E5
Stirling Ct PL5 — 15 H5
Stirling Rd PL5 — 16 A5
Stoggy La PL7 — 26 D2
Stoke Rd,
  Noss Mayo PL8 — 34 C6
Stoke Rd,
  Plymouth PL1 — 29 E2
Stokehill La PL20 — 9 A8
Stokes La PL1 — 5 E6
Stokesay Av PL6 — 18 A1
Stokingway Cl PL31 — 31 E5
Stone Barton PL7 — 26 B2
Stone Barton Cl PL7 — 26 B2
Stone Barton Rd PL7 — 26 A2
Stonehall Flats PL1 — 28 C3
Stonehenge Cl PL21 — 36 D3
Stonehouse Bri PL1 — 28 C3
Stonehouse St PL1 — 28 D3
Stony La PL18 — 6 D3
Stopford Pl PL1 — 28 C1
Stott Cl PL3 — 25 E3
Stour Cl PL3 — 25 E2
Stowe Gdns PL5 — 17 E4
Strand St PL1 — 28 C4
Strashleigh Vw PL21 — 35 C5
Stratton Walk PL2 — 17 G6
Stray Pk PL8 — 35 B1
Strode Rd PL7 — 26 D2
Stroma Cl PL3 — 12 A5
Stroud Park Rd PL2 — 23 F1
Stuart Rd PL1 — 4 A2
Sturdee Rd PL2 — 22 D3
Sugar Mill Bsns Pk
  PL9 — 30 C1
Summerfield Ct PL21 — 36 A2
Summerfields PL12 — 14 C5
Summerlands Cl PL7 — 27 G3
Summerlands Gdns
  PL7 — 27 G3
Summers Cl PL6 — 24 C1
Sunderland Cl PL9 — 30 B4
Sunningdale Rd PL12 — 14 C5
Sunny Dene PL5 — 16 A5
Sunnyside PL8 — 35 B1
Sunnyside Rd PL4 — 24 B6
Sussex Pl PL1 — 5 C6
Sussex Rd PL2 — 22 C3
Sussex St PL1 — 5 C6
Sussex Ter PL2 — 22 C3
Sutherland Rd PL4 — 4 D1
Sutton Pl PL4 — 29 H3
Sutton Rd PL4 — 5 F5
Swaindale Rd PL3 — 23 H2
Swale Cl PL3 — 24 B3
Swallows End PL31 — 31 E3
Swan Gdns PL7 — 26 D3
Swift Gdns PL5 — 17 F4
Swinburne Gdns
  PL5 — 17 F5
Sycamore Av PL4 — 30 A2
Sycamore Dr,
  Plymouth PL6 — 12 D5
Sycamore Dr,
  Torpoint PL11 — 21 F5
Sycamore Rd PL12 — 14 B4
Sycamore Way PL6 — 19 E1
Sydney Cl PL6 — 26 C4
Sydney Rd PL11 — 21 G5
Sydney St PL1 — 4 B3
Sylvian Ct PL1 — 28 D1
Symons Rd PL12 — 15 E4

Tailyour Rd PL6 — 18 A4
Talbot Gdns PL5 — 22 A1
Tamar Av PL2 — 22 B3
Tamar Ct PL12 — 15 F4
Tamar Pl PL18 — 7 F8

Tamar Science Pk
  PL6 — 18 D2
Tamar St,
  Plymouth PL1 — 28 A1
Tamar St,
  Saltash PL12 — 15 G4
Tamar St,
  Torpoint PL11 — 21 H6
Tamar Ter,
  Calstock PL18 — 7 E7
Tamar Ter,
  Gunnislake PL18 — 6 E1
Tamar Ter,
  Saltash PL12 — 15 F4
Tamar Villas PL9 — 30 D3

Tamar Vw Ind Est
  PL12 — 14 C1
Tamar Way,
  Gunnislake PL18 — 6 E2
Tamar Way,
  Plymouth PL5 — 16 D4
Tamar Wharf PL1 — 28 A1
Tamerton Cl PL5 — 16 D1
Tamerton Foliot Rd
  PL5 — 11 A6
Tamerton Rd PL6 — 12 B2
Tan St PL7 — 26 C5
Tangmere Av PL5 — 16 B1
Tannery Ct PL12 — 14 C4
Tapps La PL8 — 32 E3
Tardor Dr PL9 — 30 A4
Taunton Av PL5 — 17 E1
Taunton Pl PL5 — 17 E1
Tavistock Pl PL4 — 4 D4
Tavistock Rd,
  Crownhill PL5 — 17 H6
Tavistock Rd,
  Roborough PL6 — 12 D3
Tavistock Rd,
  Yelverton PL20 — 9 D5
Tavy Pl PL4 — 24 A4
Tavy Rd PL12 — 15 F4
Taw Cl PL3 — 25 E2
Tay Gdns PL3 — 24 D2
Taylor Cl PL12 — 14 C3
Taylor Rd PL12 — 14 C3
Teachers Cl PL31 — 31 E5
Teats Hill Flats PL4 — 29 H4
Teats Hill Rd PL4 — 5 F7
Tees Cl PL3 — 24 D2
Teign Rd PL3 — 24 C3
Telegraph Wharf PL1 — 28 C4
Telford Cres PL5 — 16 C5
Temeraire Rd PL5 — 17 G5
Tenby Rd PL5 — 15 H5
Tennyson Gdns PL5 — 17 E5
Tern Gdns PL7 — 26 D3
Terra Nova Grn PL2 — 23 E3
Tewkesbury Cl PL2 — 22 D1
Thackeray Gdns PL5 — 17 E5
Thames Gdns PL3 — 25 E3
Thanckes Cl PL11 — 21 G5
Thanckes Dr PL11 — 21 G5
The Adit PL18 — 7 F7
The Arbour PL6 — 17 H1
The Barbican PL1 — 5 E6
The Borough PL8 — 35 B2
The Bridges PL12 — 15 E5
The Broadway PL31 — 31 E3
The Chase PL21 — 36 D3
The Cleave PL10 — 33 D5
The Close PL12 — 14 C4
The Coppice PL21 — 36 A3
The Court,
  Plymouth PL6 — 12 C6
The Court,
  Saltash PL12 — 14 C4
The Crescent,
  Brixton PL8 — 32 E4
The Crescent,
  Gunnislake PL18 — 6 E1
The Crescent,
  Plymouth PL1 — 5 A5
The Crescent,
  Yelverton PL20 — 9 A6
The Dell PL7 — 26 A2
The Down PL20 — 11 C2
The Drive PL3 — 23 H1
The Elms PL3 — 22 D5
The Esplanade PL1 — 5 B7
The Fairway PL3 — 34 B5
The Fort PL10 — 33 D6
The Gallops PL12 — 14 D2
The Glade PL20 — 9 A6
The Green, Hooe PL9 — 30 B5
The Green,
  Newton Ferrers PL8 — 34 C5
The Green,
  Saltash PL12 — 14 C4
The Green,
  Torpoint PL10 — 33 D5
The Green,
  Yelverton PL20 — 9 E6
The Grove,
  Plymstock PL9 — 30 D3
The Grove,
  Stoke PL3 — 22 D5
The Groves PL21 — 36 D2
The Heathers PL6 — 12 D5
The Hedgerows PL12 — 14 B4
The Hollows PL31 — 31 H3
The Keep PL21 — 36 B2
The Kennels PL21 — 36 B2
The Knoll PL7 — 25 H2

The Lawns,
  Plymouth PL5 — 17 H5
The Lawns,
  Torpoint PL11 — 21 G5
The Limes PL6 — 18 A4
The Mead PL7 — 26 B1
The Meadows PL11 — 21 E4
The Mews,
  Plymouth PL1 — 28 C1
The Mews,
  Torpoint PL11 — 21 F6
**The Moneycentre
  Precinct** PL1 — 4 C4
The Oaks PL8 — 34 A4
The Octagon PL1 — 29 E3
The Old Laundry PL1 — 28 D2
The Old Wharf PL9 — 30 B4
The Orchard PL18 — 6 E2
The Paddocks PL18 — 6 E4
The Parade,
  Plymouth PL1 — 5 D6
The Parade,
  Torpoint PL10 — 33 B2
The Pippins PL21 — 36 A3
The Quay PL9 — 30 C3
The Retreat PL3 — 24 C1
The Ride PL9 — 30 C1
The Rivers PL12 — 15 E5
The Speares PL12 — 14 B4
The Spinney,
  Ivybridge PL21 — 36 A2
The Spinney,
  Plymouth PL7 — 27 E4
The Square,
  Gunnislake PL18 — 6 E2
The Square,
  Plymouth PL1 — 28 D2
The Square,
  Saltash PL12 — 14 C4
The Square,
  Torpoint PL10 — 33 D6
The Terrace PL1 — 28 A2
The Village PL6 — 18 C2
Theatre Ope PL1 — 28 B3
Therlow Rd PL3 — 24 B3
Thetford Gdns PL6 — 24 D1
Third Av,
  Bodmin PL31 — 31 F2
Third Av,
  Camels Head PL2 — 22 C1
Third Av,
  Plymouth PL1 — 28 C2
Thirlmere Gdns PL6 — 17 H2
Thistle Cl PL7 — 13 E5
Thorn La PL12 — 14 C3
Thorn Pk PL3 — 23 H3
Thornbury Park Av
  PL3 — 23 G2
Thornbury Rd PL6 — 19 E2
Thornhill Rd PL3 — 23 H2
Thornhill Way PL3 — 23 H2
Thornton Av PL4 — 24 A6
Thornville Ter PL9 — 30 C3
Thornyville Cl PL9 — 30 C3
Thornyville Dr PL9 — 30 C3
Thornyville Villas PL9 — 30 C3
Thurlestone Walk PL6 — 19 E6
Tillard Cl PL7 — 27 F3
Tilly Cl PL31 — 31 F6
Tin La PL4 — 5 E5
Tincombe PL12 — 14 C4
Tintagel Cres PL2 — 17 F6
Tintern Av PL4 — 30 A1
Tithe Rd PL7 — 25 H1
Tiverton Cl PL6 — 12 C5
Tobruk Rd PL12 — 14 D3
Tollbar Cl PL21 — 36 E2
Tollox Pl PL3 — 24 C4
Tom Maddock Gdns
  PL21 — 36 E3
Tor Cl PL3 — 23 H1
Tor Cres PL3 — 23 H1
Tor La PL3 — 23 G1
Tor Rd PL3 — 23 G1
Torbridge Cl PL12 — 14 C4
Torbridge Rd,
  Plymouth PL6 — 26 C2
Torbridge Rd,
  Yelverton PL20 — 8 C2
Torbryan Cl PL6 — 19 F6
Torland Rd PL3 — 23 H1
Torr Bridge Pk PL8 — 35 B2
Torr Ct PL8 — 35 C2
Torr Hill PL8 — 35 B1
Torr La PL8 — 35 C3
Torr Vw Av PL3 — 23 G2
Torre Cl PL21 — 36 F3
Torre Cotts PL8 — 35 C3
Torridge Cl PL7 — 27 E3
Torridge Rd PL7 — 26 D2

Torridge Way PL3 — 24 C3
Torver Cl PL6 — 18 D4
Tory Brook Av PL7 — 26 C3
Tory Way PL7 — 26 B2
Tothill Av PL4 — 24 A6
Tothill La PL4 — 24 A6
Tothill Rd PL4 — 29 H2
Totnes Cl PL7 — 27 F4
Tower Ct PL12 — 14 B4
Tower Vw PL12 — 14 D5
Towerfield Dr PL6 — 12 D4
Towers Cl PL6 — 19 F6
Town Farm Cl PL20 — 8 C2
Townshend Av PL2 — 22 C3
Tracey Cl PL1 — 4 B3
Trafalgar Cl PL1 — 4 E4
Trafalgar Place La PL1 — 28 C1
Trafalgar St PL4 — 4 E4
Train Rd PL9 — 34 C1
Tramway Rd PL6 — 13 E5
Transit Way PL5 — 17 F3
Treago Cl PL3 — 24 A1
Treago Gdns PL6 — 12 C4
Treby Rd PL7 — 26 D5
Treetop Cl PL12 — 14 D2
Trefusis Gdns PL3 — 23 G1
Trefusis Ter PL10 — 33 B1
Tregenna Ter PL7 — 27 G4
Tregononig Rd PL11 — 21 G6
Trehill Rd PL21 — 36 E2
Trelawney Av PL5 — 16 A5
Trelawney Cl PL11 — 21 H5
Trelawney La PL3 — 23 G3
Trelawney Pl PL5 — 16 A5
Trelawney Rd,
  Plymouth PL3 — 23 G3
Trelawney Rd,
  Saltash PL12 — 15 E4
Trelawney Rise PL11 — 21 E5
Trelawney Way PL11 — 21 E5
Trelawny Rd PL7 — 26 B2
Treloweth Cl PL2 — 23 G1
Trematon Cl PL11 — 21 F5
Trematon Dr PL21 — 36 E3
Trematon Ter PL4 — 23 H4
Trencher La PL10 — 33 A5
Trendlewood Rd PL6 — 13 E5
Trengrouse Av PL11 — 21 E5
Trent Cl PL3 — 24 B2
Trentham Cl PL6 — 12 B6
Tresillian St PL4 — 30 A2
Tresluggan Rd PL5 — 16 A6
Tretower Cl PL6 — 18 A1
Trevannion Cl PL6 — 18 A6
Trevel Vw PL11 — 21 G6
Treveneague Gdns
  PL2 — 17 G6
Treverbyn Cl PL7 — 26 B2
Treverbyn Rd PL7 — 26 B2
Trevessa Cl PL2 — 23 G1
Trevithian Ter PL3 — 23 E4
Trevithick Av PL11 — 21 F5
Trevithick Rd PL5 — 16 B5
Trevol Bsns Pk
  PL11 — 20 D5
Trevol Pl PL11 — 21 E6
Trevol Rd PL11 — 20 B6
Trevone Gdns PL12 — 17 G6
Trevorder Cl PL11 — 21 F6
Trevorder Rd PL11 — 21 E6
Trevose Way PL3 — 24 D3
Trewithy Cl PL6 — 18 A5
Trewithy Dr PL6 — 18 A5
Trinity Pl PL20 — 11 C2
Trinnaman Cl PL21 — 36 D3
Trowbridge Cl PL5 — 17 F2
Trumpers Cl PL3 — 36 A1
Truro Dr PL5 — 16 D1
Tucker Cl PL5 — 16 C6
Tuckers Cl PL8 — 35 B2
Tudor Cl PL31 — 31 E6
Tudor Ct PL12 — 15 F4
Tunnel Cotts PL6 — 19 F4
Turbill Gdns PL7 — 27 F4
Turnquay PL9 — 30 B3
Turret Gro PL4 — 24 A4
Tuxton Cl PL7 — 27 F5
Two Hills Pk PL12 — 14 B4
Two Moors Way PL21 — 36 E1
Tylney Cl PL6 — 12 C6
Tyndale Cl PL5 — 17 E5
Tything Walk PL3 — 23 H2

Ullswater Cres PL6 — 17 H2
Under Rd PL18 — 6 E2
Undercliff Rd PL9 — 30 B4
Underhay PL4 — 35 A2
Underhill Villas PL3 — 22 D5
Underlane,
  Bodmin PL31 — 31 E5

Underlane, Plympton PL7	25 H3	
Underlane, Plymstock PL9	30 D5	
Underley Cl PL6	12 C6	
Underways PL20	11 B2	
Underwood Rd PL7	26 A4	
Union Pl PL1	29 E3	
Union St PL1	5 A5	
Unity Cl PL1	19 E1	
Uphill Cl PL21	36 E2	
Upland Dr PL6	18 A1	
Upland Gdns PL9	34 D1	
Uplands PL12	15 E5	
Upper Ridings PL7	27 F2	
Upperton La PL6	13 F1	
Upton Cl PL3	24 C2	
Uxbridge Dr PL5	16 B2	

Vaagso Cl PL1 28 B2
Valiant Av PL5 16 D3
Valletort Cotts PL1 28 D1
Valletort Flats PL1 28 D2
Valletort La PL1 28 D1
Valletort Pl PL1 28 D2
Valletort Rd PL1 28 C1
Valley Dr PL9 34 C2
Valley Rd, Plymouth PL7 25 H3
Valley Rd, Saltash PL12 15 E4
Valley Rd Ind Est PL7 26 A3
Valley View Cl PL3 24 C2
Valley View Rd PL3 24 B2
Valley Vw PL6 13 E5
Vanguard Cl PL5 17 G5
Vapron Rd PL3 23 H3
Vauban Pl PL2 22 D4
Vaughan Cl PL2 23 F1
Vauxhall Ct PL4 5 E6
Vauxhall St PL1,4 5 D6
Veasypark PL9 34 C2
Venn Cl PL3 23 H2
Venn Cres PL3 23 H2
Venn Ct, Brixton PL8 32 D4
Venn Ct, Peverell PL3 23 H2
Venn Dr PL8 32 D4
Venn Gdns PL3 23 H2
Venn Gro PL3 23 H2
Venn La PL2 23 F2
Venn Way PL3 23 H2
Vermont Gdns PL2 22 C1
Verna Pl PL5 16 B4
Verna Rd PL5 16 B4
Vicarage Gdns PL5 15 H5
Vicarage Rd, Plymouth PL7 26 B3
Vicarage Rd, Torpoint PL11 21 G6
Victoria Av PL1 29 E1
Victoria Cotts, Plymouth PL6 18 C6
Victoria Cotts, Saltash PL12 15 E3
Victoria La PL12 15 F4
Victoria Pl PL2 22 C4
Victoria Rd, Plymouth PL5 16 A5
Victoria Rd, Saltash PL12 15 F4
Victoria St PL11 21 G6
Victoria Ter PL4 4 D1
Victory St PL2 22 B2
Village Dr PL6 12 D3
Villiers Cl PL9 30 D3
Vincent Way PL12 15 F5
Vine Cres PL2 23 E2
Vine Gdns PL2 23 E2
Vinery La PL9 32 A1
Vinstone Way PL5 16 B6
Violet Dr PL6 13 E4
Virginia Gdns PL2 22 D1
Vixen Tor Cl PL20 9 D5

Waddon Cl PL7 26 C1
Wadham Ter PL2 22 D3
Waggon Hill PL7 27 E4
Wain Pk PL7 26 D4
Wake St PL4 4 B1
Wakefield Av PL5 16 B5
Walcot Cl PL6 19 E3

Waldon Cl PL7 27 F2
Walker Ter PL1 5 A7
Walkham Bsns Pk PL2 17 E6
Walkham Mdws PL20 8 D3
Walkhampton Rd PL20 8 C3
Walkhampton Walk PL6 19 E5
Wall Park Cl PL7 26 D1
Wallace Rd PL7 27 E4
Walnut Cl PL7 27 F3
Walnut Dr PL7 27 G3
Walnut Gdns PL7 27 G3
Walsingham Ct PL7 27 F3
Waltacre PL8 35 B2
Walters Rd PL5 15 H5
Waltham Pl PL2 16 D6
Waltham Way PL21 36 E3
Walton Cres PL5 17 F5
Wandle Pl PL3 24 D3
Wanstead Gro PL5 16 D4
Wantage Gdns PL1 28 D2
Warburton Gdns PL5 15 H6
Ward Pl PL3 24 C3
Wardlow Cl PL6 18 A6
Wardlow Gdns PL6 18 A6
Wardour Walk PL6 12 C5
Warfelton Cres PL12 14 D4
Warfelton Gdns PL12 14 D4
Waring Rd PL6 11 C5
Warleigh Av PL2 22 B3
Warleigh Cres PL6 17 H1
Warleigh La PL2 22 B3
Warleigh Rd PL4 23 H4
Warmwell Rd PL5 16 C2
Warraton Cl PL12 14 D3
Warraton Rd PL12 14 D3
Warren Cl PL9 34 C3
Warren La, Ivybridge PL21 35 B6
Warren La, Warleigh Barton PL5 10 C4
Warren La, Wembury PL9 34 D3
Warren Pk PL6 12 D5
Warren St PL2 22 D4
Warspite Gdns PL5 17 G5
Warton Cl PL5 17 G4
Warwick Av PL5 17 F2
Warwick Orchard Cl PL5 17 E4
Wasdale Cl PL6 19 E4
Wasdale Gdns PL6 18 D4
Washbourne Cl PL1 28 B1
Waterloo Cl PL1 28 D3
Waterloo Ct PL1 28 C3
Waterloo St PL4 4 E2
Waterloo Yard Flats PL1 28 C2
Waterside PL21 36 C3
Waterslade Dr PL21 36 E3
Watson Gdns PL4 30 A1
Watson Pl PL4 30 A1
Watts Park Rd PL2 23 F1
Watts Rd PL4 24 A6
Waveney Gdns PL5 17 F3
Waverley Rd PL5 16 A4
Wavish Pk PL11 21 E5
Waycott Walk PL6 17 G1
Wayside PL21 36 C3
Wearde Rd PL12 14 D5
Weatherdon Dr PL21 36 F2
Weir Cl PL6 19 F4
Weir Gdns PL6 19 F4
Weir Rd PL6 19 F4
Welbeck Av PL4 4 D2
Well Gdns PL1 4 A4
Well Park Rd, Gunnislake PL18 6 D3
Well Park Rd, Torpoint PL11 21 G5
Welland Gdns PL3 24 C3
Wellfield Cl PL7 27 G3
Wellhay Cl PL9 32 A2
Wellington St, Devonport PL1 28 C1
Wellington St, Plymouth PL4 4 F3
Wellington St, Torpoint PL11 21 H6
Wellis Ct PL10 33 A3

Wellsbourne Pk PL3 24 A2
Wellstones Cl PL21 36 E3
Welman Rd PL10 33 C1
Welsford Av PL2 22 C4
Wembury Cotts PL31 31 G6
Wembury Mdw PL9 34 C1
Wembury Park Rd PL3 23 G2
Wembury Rd, Bodmin PL31 31 G6
Wembury Rd, Plymouth PL9 34 D1
Wenlock Gdns PL2 17 E6
Wensum Ct PL7 27 E4
Wentwood Gdns PL6 19 E3
Wentwood Pl PL6 19 E3
Wentworth Pl PL4 30 B1
Wentworth Way PL12 14 C4
Wesley Av PL3 23 H3
Wesley Pl, Mutley PL3 23 H3
Wesley Pl, Stoke PL2 22 D5
Wesley Pl PL12 15 F4
West Country Cl PL2 22 C1
West Down Rd PL2 23 E2
West End Ter PL10 33 A2
West Hill Rd PL4 24 A5
West Hoe Rd PL1 29 E3
West Malling Av PL5 16 B2
West Park Dr PL7 27 G3
West Park Hill PL7 27 E1
West St PL10 33 A2
West View Rd PL20 11 B1
Westbourne Rd PL3 23 G3
Westbourne Ter PL12 15 F3
Westbury Cl PL5 17 E2
Westbury Ter PL1 4 A3
Westcombe Cres PL9 30 C5
Westcott Cl PL6 24 A1
Westcroft Rd PL5 16 A5
Westella Rd PL20 9 F6
Westeria Ter PL3 23 F1
Western App PL1 5 A5
Western College Rd PL4 23 H4
Western Dr PL3 24 C4
Western Rd PL21 36 B3
Western Wood Way PL7 27 G3
Westfield PL7 26 D3
Westfield Av PL3 30 C5
Westhampnett Pl PL5 16 D2
Westhays Ct PL31 31 F6
Westlake Cl PL11 21 E5
Westmoor Cl PL7 27 G3
Weston Mill Dr PL5 22 B1
Weston Mill Hill PL5 16 C5
Weston Mill La PL5 16 D5
Weston Mill Rd PL5 16 B5
Weston Park Rd PL3 23 G1
Westover Cl PL7 26 B3
Westover Ind Est PL21 36 B3
Westover La PL21 36 B3
Westway PL9 30 B5
Westwood Av PL6 12 D6
Wheatridge PL7 25 H1
Whimple St PL1 5 D5
Whin Bank Rd PL5 17 G4
Whistley Down PL20 9 C6
Whitby Cres PL6 18 A5
Whitby Rd PL6 18 B5
Whitchurch Rd PL20 8 C2
White Friar La PL4 4 F4
White La PL1 5 E6
Whitefield Ter PL4 23 H6
Whiteford Rd PL3 23 H3
Whitehall Dr, Bodmin PL31 31 H3
Whitehall Dr, Yelverton PL20 11 C1
Whiterocks Pk PL18 6 A3
Whitleigh Av PL5 17 G2
Whitleigh Ct PL5 17 G2
Whitleigh Grn PL5 17 F2
Whitleigh La PL5 17 H4
Whitleigh Villas PL5 17 H4
Whitleigh Way PL5 17 F2
Whitsoncross La PL5 11 B5
Whittington St PL3 4 A2
Widdicombe Dr PL21 36 D3
Widewell La PL6 12 C5

Widewell Rd PL6 12 C5
Widey Ct PL6 18 A5
Widey Hill PL8 34 D5
Widey La PL6 18 A5
Widey Vw PL3 24 A2
Wilburt Rd PL6 25 E1
Wilderness Rd PL3 23 H4
Wilkinson Rd PL5 22 A1
Williams Av PL4 30 B1
Willow Cl PL3 25 F3
Willow Cotts PL7 26 B4
Willow Ct PL6 25 F1
Willow Grn PL12 14 C4
Willow Walk PL6 19 F1
Willowby Gdns PL20 9 F7
Willowby Pk PL20 9 F7
Wills Cl PL6 11 D5
Wilmot Gdns PL5 17 G4
Wilson Cres PL2 23 E3
Wilton Rd PL1 28 D2
Wilton St PL1 28 D1
Winchester Gdns PL5 16 D1
Windermere Cres PL6 18 A2
Windmill Hill PL12 15 E4
Windsor Cl PL21 36 E3
Windsor La PL12 15 E4
Windsor Pl PL1 5 C6
Windsor Rd PL3 24 C2
Windsor Ter PL11 21 H5
Windsor Villas PL1 5 C6
Wingfield Rd PL3 23 E5
Wingfield Way PL3 23 E5
Winnicott Cl PL6 11 D5
Winnow Cl PL31 31 E6
Winsbury Ct PL6 18 A5
Winstanley Walk PL3 24 D3
Winston Av PL4 4 C2
Winstone La PL8 32 E4
Witham Gdns PL3 24 C3
Woburn Ter PL9 30 C3
Wollaton Gro PL5 16 D3
Wolrige Av PL7 27 E3
Wolrige Way PL7 27 E4
Wolsdon St PL1 29 E2
Wolseley Cl PL2 22 D3
Wolseley Rd, Camels Head PL2,5 22 B1
Wolseley Rd, Riverside PL5 15 G5
Wolverwood Cl PL7 27 F5
Wolverwood La PL7 26 D5
Wombwell Cres PL2 22 B2
Wood Acre PL12 14 B2
Wood Cl PL12 14 B3
Wood Pk, Ivybridge PL21 36 D1
Wood Pk, Plymouth PL6 19 G4
Wood Vw PL31 31 G5
Woodburn Cl PL7 26 B2
Woodbury Gdns PL5 17 E3
Woodcock Cl PL10 33 C1
Woodend Rd PL6 13 E5
Woodfield Cres PL7 26 E3
Woodford Cl PL7 25 G2
Woodford Cres PL7 25 H2
Woodford Grn PL7 25 H2
Woodford Rd, Glenholt PL6 12 D6
Woodford Rd, Woodford Ter PL7 26 A3
Woodhey Rd PL2 22 D2
Woodland Av PL31 31 G3
Woodland Cl, Gunnislake PL18 6 E1
Woodland Cl, Ivybridge PL21 36 B3
Woodland Dr PL7 26 A4
Woodland Rd, Cadleigh Park PL21 35 D4
Woodland Rd, Colebrook PL7 26 B2
Woodland Rd, Ivybridge PL21 36 A2
Woodland Ter, Ivybridge PL21 36 B3
Woodland Ter, Plymouth PL4 24 A5
Woodland Way, Gunnislake PL18 6 E1

Woodland Way, Torpoint PL11 21 F5
Woodlands, Bodmin PL31 31 F4
Woodlands, Ivybridge PL21 36 B3
Woodlands Ct PL5 16 D3
Woodlands End PL6 18 D1
Woodlands La PL6 19 F5
Woodside Av PL9 30 C5
Woodside Cl PL21 36 D3
Woodside Ct PL7 26 C4
Woodside La PL4 24 A5
Woodstock Gdns PL5 16 A5
Woodview Pk PL31 31 G5
Woodville Cl PL2 22 D2
Woodville Rd PL2 22 D2
Woodway PL31 31 F4
Woolacombe Rd PL20 11 D2
Woolcombe La PL21 36 D3
Woollcombe Av PL7 26 D5
Woolms Mdw PL21 36 A3
Woolwell Cres PL6 12 D4
Woolwell Dr PL6 12 D5
Woolwell Rd PL6 12 D5
Wordsworth Cres PL2 22 C1
Wordsworth Rd PL2 22 C1
Worthele Cl PL21 36 A3
Wren Gdns PL7 26 A2
Wrens Gate PL31 31 E3
Wright Cl PL1 28 A2
Wrights La PL8 34 B5
Wycliffe Rd PL3 24 C4
Wye Gdns PL3 25 E2
Wykeham Dr PL2 22 D1
Wyndham La PL1 29 E2
Wyndham Sq PL1 29 E2
Wyndham St East PL1 4 A3
Wyndham St West PL1 29 E2
Wyoming Cl PL3 24 D2
Wythburn Gdns PL6 19 E4

Yardley Gdns PL6 19 E3
Yarrow Mead PL9 32 B1
Yarrowpoole Cotts PL9 32 B1
Yealm Pk PL8 35 A2
Yealm Rd PL8 34 A5
Yealm View Rd PL8 34 C5
Yealmbury Hill PL8 35 B1
Yealmbury Villas PL8 35 B1
Yealmpstone Cl PL7 27 E5
Yealmpstone Dr PL7 27 F5
Yeats Cl PL5 17 F4
Yellow Tor Ct PL12 14 B3
Yellowtor Rd PL12 14 B3
Yelverton Cl PL5 16 B3
Yeo Cl PL3 24 C3
Yeolland La PL21 36 D3
Yeolland Pk PL21 36 D3
Yeomans Way PL7 27 E5
Yewdale Gdns PL6 18 D4
Yonder St PL9 30 B5
York Pl PL2 22 C5
York Rd, Plymouth PL5 22 B1
York Rd, Torpoint PL11 21 G5
York St PL1 28 B2
York Ter PL2 22 C5
Youldon Way PL20 8 D3

Zion Pl PL21 36 C3
Zion St PL1 5 C6

www.ESTATE-PUBLICATIONS.co.uk

Redbooks - showing the way

For the latest publication list, prices and to order online please visit our website.

OFFICIAL TOURIST MAPS and TOURIST MAPS
(Official Tourist Maps are shown in **Bold** Type)

-	Kent to Cornwall 1:460,000
1	**South East England** 1:200,000
101	**Kent & East Sussex** 1:150,000
102	**Sussey & Surrex Downs** 1:150,000
103	South East England Leisure Map 1:200,000
104	**Sussex** 1:150,000
2	**Southern England** 1:200,000
201	Isle of Wight 1:50,000
3	**Wessex** 1:200,000
301	Dorset 1:150,000
4	**Devon & Cornwall** 1:200,000
401	**Cornwall** 1:180,000
402	**Devon** 1:200,000
403	**Dartmoor & South Devon Coast** 1:100,000
404	**Exmoor & North Devon** 1:100,000
5	Greater London (M25 Map) 1:80,000
6	**East Anglia** 1:200,000
7	**Chilterns & Thames Valley** 1:200,000
8	**Cotswolds, Severn Valley** 1:200,000
302	The Cotswolds 1:110,000
9	Wales 1:250,000
10	**The Shires of Middle England** 1:250,000
11	**The Mid Shires** (Staffs, Shrops, etc.) 1:200,000
111	**Peak District** 1:100,000
12	Snowdonia 1:125,000
13	**Yorkshire** 1:200,000
131	**Yorkshire Dales** 1:125,000
132	**North Yorkshire Moors** 1:125,000
4	**North West England** 1:200,000
41	**Isle of Man** 1:60,000
5	**North Pennines & Lakes** 1:200,000
51	Lake District 1:75,000
6	**Borders of Scotland & England** 1:200,000
7	**Burns Country** 1:200,000
8	Heart of Scotland 1:200,000
81	**Greater Glasgow** 1:150,000
82	**Edinburgh & The Lothians** 1:150,000
83	**Isle of Arran** 1:63,360
84	**Fife (Kingdom of)** 1:100,000
9	**Loch Lomond** 1:150,000

191	**Argyll, The Isles & Loch Lomond** 1:275,000
20	**Perthshire** 1:150,000
21	**Fort William, Ben Nevis, Glen Coe** 1:185,000
211	Iona and Mull 1:10,000 / 1:115,000
22	**Grampian Highlands** 1:185,000
23	**Loch Ness & Aviemore** 1:150,000
24	**Skye & Lochalsh** 1:130,000
25	**Argyll & The Isles** 1:200,000
26	**Caithness & Sutherland** 1:185,000
27	**Western Isles** 1:125,000
28	**Orkney & Shetland** 1:128,000 }same map
28	**Shetland & Orkney** 1:128,000
30	**Highlands of Scotland** 1:275,000
92	England & Wales 1:650,000
93	Scotland 1:500,000
94	Historic Scotland 1:500,000
95	Scotland (Homelands of the Clans)
99	Great Britain 1:1,100,000
99	Great Britain (Flat) 1:1,100,000
100	British Isles 1:1,100,000

EUROPEAN LEISURE MAPS

Europe 1:3,100,000
Cross Channel Visitors' Map 1:530,000
France 1:1,000,000
Germany 1:1,000,000
Ireland 1:625,000
Italy 1:1,000,000
Netherlands, Belgium & Luxembourg 1:600,000
Spain & Portugal 1:1,000,000

WORLD MAPS

World Map - Political (Folded) 1:29,000,000
World Map - Political (Flat in Tube) 1:29,000,000
World Travel Adventure Map (Folded) 1:29,000,000
World Travel Adventure Map (Flat in Tube) 1:29,000,000

ESTATE PUBLICATIONS, Bridewell House, Tenterden, Kent. TN30 6EP
Tel: 01580 764225   Fax: 01580763720   Email: sales@estate-publications.co.uk

www.ESTATE-PUBLICATIONS.co.uk

Redbooks - showing the way

For the latest publication list, prices and to order online please visit our website.

LOCAL and SUPER RED BOOKS
(Super Red Books are shown in **Bold** Type)
Aldershot & Camberley
Alfreton & Belper
Andover
Ashford & Tenterden
Aylesbury & Tring
Bangor & Caernarfon
Barnstaple & Bideford
Basildon & Billericay
Basingstoke & Alton
Bath & Bradford-upon-Avon
Bedford
Birmingham
Bodmin & Wadebridge
Bournemouth
Bracknell & Wokingham
Brentwood
Brighton
Bristol
Bromley (London Borough)
Burton-upon-Trent & Swadlincote
Bury St. Edmunds & Stowmarket
Cambridge
Cannock & Rugeley
Cardiff
Cardiff City & Bay Visitors Map (Sheet Map)
Carlisle & Penrith
Chelmsford
Chester
Chesterfield & Dronfield
Chichester & Bognor Regis
Chippenham & Calne
Coatbridge & Airdrie
Colchester & Clacton-on-Sea
Corby & Kettering
Coventry
Crawley & Mid Sussex
Crewe
Derby
Dundee & St. Andrews
Eastbourne
Edinburgh
Exeter & Exmouth
Falkirk & Grangemouth
Fareham & Gosport
Flintshire Towns
Folkestone & Dover
Glasgow
Gloucester & Cheltenham
Gravesend & Dartford
Grays & Thurrock
Great Yarmouth & Lowestoft
Grimsby & Cleethorpes
Guildford & Woking
Hamilton & Motherwell
Harlow & Bishops Stortford
Harrogate & Knaresborough
Hastings & Bexhill
Hereford
Hertford & Waltham Cross
High Wycombe

Huntingdon & St. Neots
Ipswich
Isle of Man
Isle of Wight Towns
Kendal & Windermere
Kidderminster
Kingston upon Hull
Lancaster & Morecambe
Leicester
Lincoln
Llandudno & Colwyn Bay
Luton & Dunstable
Macclesfield & Wilmslow
Maidstone
Mansfield
Medway & Gillingham
Milton Keynes
New Forest Towns
Newbury & Thatcham
Newport & Chepstow
Newquay & Perranporth
Newtown & Welshpool
Northampton
Northwich & Winsford
Norwich
Nottingham
Nuneaton & Bedworth
Oxford & Abingdon
Penzance & St. Ives
Perth
Peterborough
Plymouth
Portsmouth
Reading & Henley-on-Thames
Redditch & Bromsgrove
Reigate & Mole Valley
Rhyl & Prestatyn
Rugby
St. Albans, Welwyn & Hatfield
St. Austell & Lostwithiel
Salisbury & Wilton
Scarborough & Whitby
Scunthorpe
Sevenoaks
Shrewsbury
Sittingbourne & Faversham
Slough, Maidenhead & Windsor
Southampton
Southend-on-Sea
Stafford
Stevenage & Letchworth
Stirling & Alloa
Stoke-on-Trent
Stroud & Nailsworth
Swansea
Swindon
Tamworth & Lichfield
Taunton & Bridgwater
Telford & Newport
Tenby & Saundersfoot
Thanet & Canterbury
Torbay

Trowbridge & Frome
Truro & Falmouth
Tunbridge Wells & Tonbridge
Warwick & Royal Leamington Spa
Watford & Hemel Hempstead
Wellingborough & Rushden
Wells & Glastonbury
Weston-super-Mare
Weymouth & Dorchester
Winchester
Wolverhampton (Sheet Map)
Worcester
Workington & Whitehaven
Worthing & Littlehampton
Wrexham
York

COUNTY RED BOOKS
(Town Centre Maps)
Bedfordshire
Berkshire
Buckinghamshire
Cambridgeshire
Cheshire
Cornwall
Cumbria
Derbyshire
Devon
Dorset
Essex
Gloucestershire
Hampshire
Herefordshire
Hertfordshire
Kent
Leicestershire & Rutland
Lincolnshire
Norfolk
Northamptonshire
Nottinghamshire
Oxfordshire
Shropshire
Somerset
Staffordshire
Suffolk
Surrey
Sussex (East)
Sussex (West)
Warwickshire
Wiltshire
Worcestershire

EUROPEAN STREET MAPS
Calais & Boulogne Shoppers Map (Sheet Map)
Dieppe Shoppers Map (Sheet Map)
North French Towns Street Atlas

ESTATE PUBLICATIONS, Bridewell House, Tenterden, Kent. TN30 6EP
Tel: 01580 764225   Fax: 01580763720   Email: sales@estate-publications.co.uk